The Wellness Mama
COOKBOOK

special gift for you...

Hi!

Thanks for purchasing the Wellness Mama Cookbook! I'm so excited you've taken this small step to improve your family's health through a real food diet. As a "thank you" for purchasing my cookbook, and to help make your "Wellness Lifestyle" transition easier, I've created some bonus videos and information just for you.

You can download it for free at:
http://WellnessMamaCookbook.com/Bonus

Thanks for reading and have a healthy week!

Warmly,
Katie, the Wellness Mama

The Wellness Mama Cookbook: Simple Recipes for Healthier Families

ISBN 978-1-63456-000-9 (hardcover)

Printed in the United States of America

Published by: Wellness Media
PO Box 160
Rockfield, KY 42274

Photographers: Katie Wellness Mama, Suzanne Perazzini, Mandy Whitley Photography
Contributing Editors: Olivia Spears and Julia Romano
Design: Carrie Medeiros

disclaimer:

To my husband and children

I love you more than words can express
and you are the reason I write, cook and care.

To my parents

Thank you for your support and for teaching me
to question everything and forge my own path.

To you

Thank you for reading and for caring about real food and the
future for next generations. I truly believe that we can (and
must) make these changes now to protect future generations.

And to those in the world who don't have access to quality food

At least 10% of author's royalties on this book are donated
to charities that work to provide clean water and sustainable
food sources for those in need around the world.

"You can do no great things,
only small things with great love."

- Mother Theresa

table
of contents

recipes:

intro:

When my oldest child was just six weeks old, I was sitting in the doctor's office for a follow-up appointment and nursing him while I waited to see the doctor. My birth hadn't been what I had hoped it would be and being back at the doctor's office was a vivid reminder of that.

In a way, I felt like I had failed. My water broke before contractions started and I went immediately to the hospital where I was put "on the clock." After about 12 hours of natural labor, I was put on a 2-hour timetable at only six centimeters dilated. The on-call doctor wanted to do a c-section at only 12 hours after my water broke even though there was no sign of infection or stress to the baby. I later found out that the on-call doctor had the highest c-section rate in our city.

I agreed to start pitocin to avoid the c-section if possible and ended up needing an epidural when the pain started causing me to blackout.

In hindsight, there were so many things that I would change about that birth but at the same time, I wouldn't change it for the world. I learned a lot about myself that day, I met my son, and my bond with my husband became even stronger. That day ignited a strength and passion I didn't know I was capable of and I got what I called the "mother lion" instinct as soon as I saw my son.

Six weeks after giving birth I was still reflecting on the many emotions associated with birth and learning the ropes of caring for a newborn as I sat nursing my little guy and mindlessly flipping through a magazine.

My finger stopped on a page of the magazine with a picture of a cute baby (something new moms tend to do), and I read the first paragraph of that article. I came to a sentence that made me stop in my tracks:

"For the first time in two centuries, the current generation of children in America may have shorter life expectancies than their parents."

I re-read that sentence and looked down at my perfect, healthy baby and the contrast hit me like a bolt of lightning. My mother lion instinct kicked in again and every cell in my body rebelled against that statement.

At that moment, I decided that statistics like that weren't good enough for our children!

At that moment, I developed a passion for changing those statistics and empowering other parents to do the same.

I realized that parents would be the ones to make these changes for several reasons:

1. We are raising the future generation. We can teach them healthy habits and healthy attitudes about food so that they aren't doomed to suffer this future
2. We control about 80% of the food budget and can vote with our dollars to change the food industry
3. We care more about the future generation because they aren't just statistics to us; they are our precious children.

Since that day eight years ago, I've been on a journey to improve the health of my family and to help other moms improve their family's health as well.

In the process, I've identified my own health struggles and worked to overcome them. I'm not perfect. My family isn't perfect. I am very much a work in progress, but I think we all are. This book is part of my desire to share my own journey and what I've learned so that other families won't have to struggle with the same learning curve I had to beat.

Five kids later, I've learned a little about parenting, a lot about cooking and cleaning, and a lot about myself.

I was recently diagnosed with an autoimmune thyroid disease called Hashimoto's thyroiditis. Essentially, my body is attacking my thyroid and I have several nodules on my thyroid that are (thankfully) now shrinking. It took years for me to get answers but I now know that my years of processed foods, high stress and lack of sleep created a prefect breeding ground for this autoimmune disease. A nourishing diet, however, is helping my body reverse these problems.

Through this struggle, I've realized how nourishing food is absolutely essential to health and how the standard diet is failing many of us!

You thought you were buying a cookbook, but my mission is to recruit you to change the future for our children! I hope you join me on this mission and that together we can make lasting changes.

Happy reading and happy cooking!

Warmly,
Katie
"the Wellness Mama"

"It is health that is real
wealth and not pieces
of gold and silver."

- Mahatma Gandhi

It doesn't take a scientist to notice that there are a lot of health problems in our world today.

Every day, there are new reports of rising rates of disease, obesity, cancers and other problems. Most alarmingly, these rates are rising the most quickly in younger population groups and even children.

Certainly, there are a large variety of factors that are contributing to these problems but food plays a tremendous role. Our foods aren't what they once were and many of the foods we are told are healthy are actually making us sick.

Among the top three offenders: processed and modified grains, processed omega-6 vegetable oils and sugar.

{ the problem of grains }

Grains contain Phytic Acid, a mineral blocker that prevents absorption of calcium, magnesium, iron, copper and zinc. Phytic acid is found in the bran of all grains as well as the outer coating of seeds and nuts. After grains became more mainstream during the agricultural revolution, they were allowed to sit in the fields for several weeks before threshing. This exposed the harvest to the elements and allowed the grains to sprout. Evidence shows that sprouting increases the content of many important vitamins, and breaks down the phytic acid.

Grains today however, are not sprouted and are consumed in much larger quantities than ever before. The presence of the phytates blocks the absorption of calcium, a risk factor for osteoporosis and other bone-related problems. Unfortunately, many doctors prescribe a low-fat, high-fiber diet and a calcium supplement for those with osteoporosis. The calcium isn't being absorbed, however, because the phytates block its uptake.

Perhaps you noticed the general consensus among medical professionals that grains are not only healthy, but the necessary foundation of our diet (solidly nestled at the base of our "food pyramid"). It's trendy to acknowledge that processed grains are bad but to deify those "healthy whole grains" that supposedly provide the bulk of our nutrition in just 6-11 servings a day!

The sad truth is that grain consumption, especially in the forms found today, are a blatant departure from the way humans have eaten for most of our history. Relatively recently, the ability to grow and process grains more easily allowed more people to afford grain products like flour, a "luxury" previously reserved for the wealthy. But remember: accessibility does not mean our bodies can handle grains or that we can function optimally while consuming them.

Besides the phytic acid, which strips your body of the ability to properly absorb nutrients, another serious disadvantage to grain consumption is the astronomical spike in insulin production. Insulin production is an important process for storing nutrients and processing glucose in the bloodstream, but our bodies simply can't handle the insulin requirements we throw at them with the carb load we consume these days.

Let's take a trip back to freshman Biology, shall we? When carbohydrates enter the body (regardless of the source) they are eventually broken down into glucose. Any extra glucose floating around in the body that we are not immediately using is stored as fat by insulin. This is a natural response of our bodies, and it has allowed humans to survive for thousands of years, even through famine. If we aren't using the fuel now, our bodies store it for future use in the form of fat.

Fortunately for us, we are not commonly faced with famine, but because of this, we don't often get the chance to use up these excess fat stores, so the fat accumulates. If the carbohydrate consumption is excessive (milkshake, anyone?) the body throws in the added bonus of cortisol and adrenaline hormone production to handle the extra load. This whole hormonal song and dance does the tango on the body's endocrine and immune systems and creates inflammation in the body. When this happens regularly over a long period of time, it takes a very serious toll on the body.

It is no secret that the United States is facing a very real epidemic of insulin sensitivity, Type 2 Diabetes, insulin resistance, and obesity. If the corresponding rates of disease and weight gain with grain consumption over the last 130 years aren't enough to convince you, consider this: when ground into flour, the surface area of a grain is increased to 10,000 times the surface area of the grain itself. The resulting high-starch food is biologically similar to consuming pure table sugar. Consider the fact that flour is often mixed with sugar to create recipes (or used to make wall-paper paste, your choice) and you have a virtual diabetic coma in a bowl (or can).

In the last 130 years of increased grain consumption, chronic disease rates have skyrocketed, fertility has fallen and the average weight of the population has steadily risen. The more consumption of grains rose, the more fertility rates fell. Research from the University of Missouri found that the average sperm count of American males has dropped 50% since the 1930s. To add insult to, well, impotence, testicle size tends to have an inverse relationship with grain consumption.

Sounds bad enough to me, but there are still a few villains left in this story! Behold gluten and lectins! These two are the Bonnie and Clyde of digestive health.

Gluten is a sticky, water-soluble protein that is found in your favorite grains (wheat, rye, barley, etc). Grains like corn, rice and oats have similar proteins that cause problems over time. Gluten and similar grain-based proteins can cause problems by breaking down the microvilli in your small intestine, eventually letting particles of your food leech into your blood stream (a lovely term called "leaky gut syndrome") causing allergies, digestive disturbances or autoimmune problems.

Gluten's sidekicks, the posse of Lectins, are mild toxins that inhibit the repair of the GI track. Lectins are not broken down in the digestive process and bind to receptors in the intestine, allowing them and other food particles to leech into your bloodstream. Nothing like pre-digested food circulating the blood stream! The body views these lectins and the food they bring with them as dangerous invaders and initiates an immune response to get rid of them. This immune response to particles of common foods explains the allergy-creating potential of grains.

Once they have wrecked your gut, Gluten and Lectin move their destructive dance to the gallbladder. The Gallbladder releases bile salts that help break down and properly digest foods. When the intestines are damaged, the chemical responsible for starting this bile secretion is not released. Bile backs up in the gall bladder, and cholesterol that is left there crystallizes into little "stones" that are usually surgically removed with the rest of the gall bladder. Talk about cutting off the nose to spite the face!

Grains can block certain nutrients, cause weight gain and infertility, but don't they still have nutrients? Unfortunately, grains do not have the nutritional profile that all the granola-pushing commercials of late make them out to have. It makes much more sense to get your nutrients from foods like vegetables, fruits, proteins and healthy fats, which offer much higher nutrient profiles without the drawbacks.

"But what about the fiber in grains?" Some might ask "and what about the vitamins?"

You know what else is a good source of fiber, vitamins and minerals? Vegetables.
You know what also has MORE fiber, vitamins and minerals? Vegetables.

You know what also doesn't have the potential to cause gut damage (in most cases)? Vegetables.

If we are feeling really brave, we can even add in foods like liver, broth, fermented vegetables and eggs (if tolerated) and blow the nutrition profile of grains completely out of the water.

do we need grains?
Let's break down the reasons that we are often told that we need grains: fiber, vitamins and minerals. Do grains really have spectacular amounts of these substances that are hard to find elsewhere?

fiber:

Fiber is often suggested for its supposed ability to move things along in the digestive system. Researchers explained that high fiber foods accomplish this when they puncture the cells of the gastrointestinal track, which ruptures their outer covering and creates a layer of lubricating mucus to help heal the intestines.

We do need a certain amount of the right kind of fiber, but this fiber can be easily obtained from vegetables and fruit without the need for additional insoluble fiber from grains.

vitamins and minerals:

Grains are often suggested for their vitamin and mineral content, specifically for B-vitamins and Magnesium. Just as with fiber, these things can be easily found in other foods. For example, let's compare some of the most common nutrients that are found in grains with levels of the same nutrients found in vegetables:

Thiamin: Vegetables contain more than grains
Riboflavin: Vegetables win again
Niacin: and again

Folate: and again
Iron: and again
Magnesium: and again
Selenium: A tie between some veggies and grains

In other words, vegetables contain more vitamins and minerals per serving than grains do, without the potential for harm.

the bottom line:

Gluten is not a food group.

Grains do contain some nutrients, but these nutrients can be found in larger amounts in fruits, vegetables and meats/fats.

I will agree with many nutritionists that going gluten free isn't going to do much good if you just replace the gluten with gluten free processed foods. These gluten free processed alternatives often have more sugar and chemical substances to balance out the lack of gluten.

If, however, you replace the gluten containing foods (and all grains) with vegetables, fruits, fermented probiotic-rich foods, homemade broths, organ meats and humanely raised animal meats, you will not be missing out on vitamins and minerals. In fact, according to the latest statistics I've seen for food consumption in the US, you'll be head and shoulders above the rest of the population on vitamin and mineral intake.

Since grains are often fortified with additional nutrients, it is important to make sure that you are eating a varied and nutrient rich diet when you go grain free.

It all boils down to this: Grains are not healthy and they are toxic to the body. That is the way they were designed. The non-digestible proteins that wreak havoc in our system allow grains to pass un-harmed through the intestines of animals and emerge victoriously in a pile of fertilizer at the other end. Good for the grains-bad for us! Studies have shown, and I have seen in my own health, that a no-grain diet can lower cholesterol, lower blood pressure, reduce inflammation, promote weight loss, alleviate dermatitis or acne, end digestive disturbances, increase fertility and dramatically improve energy levels.

Did she just say no-grain? That means pasta, bread, pastries, desserts, rolls, crackers, etc! (I would actually add white potatoes, corn, and any forms of "whole grains" to that list.) Say it isn't so!

Trust me, I like them too and used to live on them! From personal experience I can tell you that there is no comparison between how you feel when you don't eat grains and when you do. I realize that you probably like grains a lot, and that your doctor probably even encourages you to eat them. I understand that the idea of giving them up might sound absurd or even impossible. I also know that giving up the grains is one of the best things you can do for your health.

If you aren't willing to make the full plunge to grain-free, at least consider consuming properly prepared grains to reduce the chance of these problems.

soaking, sprouting and fermenting:

Traditional cultures around the world where grains were consumed regularly or in large amounts found ways to reduce the harmful components of grains through methods like soaking, sprouting and fermenting.

These methods are designed to do what our body can't and break down the anti-nutrients (gluten, lectin, phytic acid, etc.) in grains so that they are more digestible to us. Evidence shows that by using an acidic medium in liquid to soak the grains, a constructive environment to let them sprout, or a process like sourdough fermentation to alter the chemical make-up of the grain can make the nutrients in grains much more bioavailable and reduce the anti-nutrient properties.

Traditional cultures around the world, from primitive African tribes to Russian villages to ancient European societies have used various methods of soaking, sprouting and fermenting to reduce the harmful components of grains.

are soaked, sprouted and fermented grains healthy?

From a nutrient perspective, grains prepared in these ways do have much higher nutrient levels and lower anti-nutrient levels than grains that are just ground into flour and baked, but should they be eaten?

Soaking and sprouting reduces phytate slightly but not by a significant amount. When a grain is heated, it destroys phytase (which reduces phytic acid) so the phytic acid will remain intact.

When grains are allowed to sprout, enzyme inhibitors are reduced or eliminated, so those who consume grains should seriously consider using only sprouted versions.

Soaking and sprouting reduce the lectins in grains slightly but the amount that it is reduced varies by type of grain. Sprouting and soaking reduce gluten slightly but not completely and even a small amount of gluten can be damaging to some people.

Adding fermentation to the mix reduces the harmful properties even more, but does not completely render them harmless. And remember insulin? Even sprouted, soaked and fermented grains cause a spike in insulin and can inhibit weight loss and lead to other health problems if eaten in large amounts.

so, should we eat them?

Soaking, sprouting, and fermentation do improve the nutrient profile of what is otherwise a harmful food, but this still doesn't mean that grains, even prepared using one of these methods, are healthy or that we need to consume them.

If you are going to consume any grains, it would definitely be better to prepare them in one of these ways (or all three!) to make them less harmful to your body.

In short, I don't recommend grain consumption at all, even if they are properly prepared, as they aren't an exceptional nutrient source and they have harmful properties.

vegetable oils

Aside from "healthy whole grains," vegetable oils and margarine are some of the most misunderstood and over-recommended foods in the health community. You've probably heard these referred to as "heart healthy oils," a good alternative to those "artery clogging saturated fats."

These oils are supposed to help lower cholesterol and blood pressure, increase weight loss, and somehow improve overall health.

Only one problem...again, science doesn't back these claims up!

what are vegetable oils/margarine?

Vegetable oils (and margarine, made from these oils) are oils extracted from seeds like the rapeseed (canola oil), soybean (soybean oil), corn, sunflower, safflower, etc. They were practically non-existent in our diets until the early 1900s when new chemical processes allowed them to be extracted. Vegetable oils are now found in practically every processed food, from salad dressing to mayonnaise to conventional nuts and seeds.

These oils are also some of the most harmful substances you can put into your body! Unlike butter or coconut oil, these vegetable oils can't be extracted just by pressing or separating naturally. They must be chemically removed, deodorized, and altered. These are some of the most chemically altered foods in our diets.

how vegetable oils are made

Vegetable oils are manufactured in a factory, usually from genetically modified crops that have been heavily treated with pesticides.

Take, for instance, the common Canola oil: the beauty queen of the vegetable oil industry. It is made from rapeseed, but was given its cute n' cuddly name in the 1980s as part of a marketing effort organized by a conference on mono-saturates.

Rapeseed (and rapeseed oil) contains high amounts of the toxic erucic acid, which is poisonous to the body. Canola oil is made from an altered, hybrid version of rapeseed called Low Erucic Acid Rapeseed (LEAR). It is commonly genetically modified and treated with high levels of pesticides.

The oil is produced by heating the rapeseed and processing it with a petroleum solvent to extract the oil. Then another process of heat and addition of acid is used to remove nasty solids (wax) that occur during the first processing.

At this point, the newly created canola oil must be treated with more chemicals to improve color and separate the different parts. Finally, since all these chemical processes have given it a harsh smell, it must be chemically deodorized to be palatable.

If the canola oil is going to be made into shortening or margarine, it undergoes an additional process called hydrogenation to make it solid at cold temperatures. Unlike saturated fats (butter, coconut oil, etc.) vegetable oils are not naturally solid at these temperatures and must be hydrogenated to accomplish this. During this process of hydrogenation, those lovely trans fats we've heard so much about are created.

Nothing like petroleum-produced, overheated, oxidized, and chemically deodorized salad dressing for dinner...yum.

Compare this process to how butter is made. Step 1: milk cow. Step 2: let cream separate naturally. Step 3: skim off cream. Step 4: shake cream until it becomes butter.

chemicals and additives in vegetable oils and fats

Since vegetable oils are chemically produced, it's not really surprising that they contain harmful chemicals. Most vegetable oils and their products contain BHA and BHT (Butylated Hydroxyanisole and Butylated Hydroxytoluene), which are artificial antioxidants that help prevent food from oxidizing or spoiling too quickly.

These chemicals have been shown to produce potential cancer causing compounds in the body, and have also been linked to liver/kidney damage, immune problems, infertility or sterility, high cholesterol, and behavioral problems in children.

Vegetable oils also contain residues of the pesticides and chemicals used in their growth and manufacture and most often come from genetically modified sources.

history of vegetable oil production and consumption

Vegetable oil was practically non-existent in its current form in the early 1900s. Until that time, most people got their fats from animal sources like meat, tallow, lard, butter, cream, etc. The overall amount of fat consumed since then has not changed much (it has decreased slightly) but the type of fat has changed dramatically.

Vegetable oil use didn't increase much until the 1950s, when a governmental campaign was launched to convince people to eat vegetable oils and margarine and avoid "artery clogging saturated fats." Today, people consume, on average, about 70 pounds of vegetable oils throughout the year. I wonder what 70 pounds of a "food" that was previously non-existent in human consumption might do to our health?

Add to this the fact that the animals we eat are also often fed genetically modified, pesticide treated seeds and grains (instead of their natural foods, like grass) and the amount of omega-6 rich oils and seeds in our diet is really high!

But do these vegetable oils reduce the risk of disease and do saturated fats increase it?

All one has to do is look at the statistics to know that it isn't true. Butter consumption at the turn of the century was 18 pounds per person per year, and the use of vegetable oils almost nonexistent. Yet cancer and heart disease were rare. Today butter consumption hovers just above 4 pounds per person per year while vegetable oil consumption has soared–and cancer and heart disease are endemic.

what's wrong with vegetable oils?

There are many problems with vegetable oil consumption, and in my opinion, no amount is safe. To understand why, let's look at a few of the biggest problems with vegetable oils:

Our Bodies Aren't Meant to Consume Them!

The fat content of the human body is about 97% saturated and monounsaturated fat, with only 3% polyunsaturated fats. Vegetable oils contain very high levels of polyunsaturated fats, and these oils have replaced many of the saturated fats in our diets since the 1950s.

The body needs fats for rebuilding cells and hormone production, but it has to use the building blocks we give it. When we give it a high concentration of polyunsaturated fats instead of the fats it needs, it has no choice but to incorporate these fats into our cells during cell repair and creation.

The problem is that polyunsaturated fats are highly unstable and oxidize easily in the body (if they haven't already oxidized during processing or by light exposure while sitting on the grocery store shelf). These oxidized fats cause inflammation and mutation in cells.

In arterial cells, these mutations cause inflammation that can clog arteries. When these fats are incorporated into skin cells, their mutation causes skin cancer. (This is why people often get the most dangerous forms of skin cancer in places where they are never exposed to the sun).

When these oils are incorporated into cells in reproductive tissue, some evidence suggests that this can spur problems like endometriosis and Polycystic Ovarian Syndrome (PCOS). In short, the body is made up of saturated and monounsaturated fats, and it needs these for optimal health. Feeding it polyunsaturated fats instead is harmful.

The body needs Omega-3 and Omega-6 fats, the 2 polyunsaturated fats, in balance, preferably a 1:1 ratio. Most people, however, consume a much higher amount of Omega-6 fats... and this can lead to problems.

Vegetable oils are one of the main culprits: they contain a very high concentration of Omega-6 fatty acids. Omega-6 fats are easily oxidized with heat or light exposure. This is another reason that when these types of fats/oils are incorporated into tissue like skin cells, the heat and light from sun exposure can increase skin cancer risk.

In one study, Dr. Vivienne Reeve, PhD, Head of the Photobiology Research Group at the University of Sydney, irradiated a group of mice while feeding different groups of them polyunsaturated and saturated fats. She discovered that the mice that consumed only saturated fat were totally protected from skin cancer. Those in the polyunsaturated fat group quickly developed skin cancers. Later in the study, the mice in the saturated fat group were given polyunsaturated fats. Skin cancers quickly developed in those mice as well.

The 3% of our body that is made up of polyunsaturated fats is approximately half Omega-3 fatty acids and half Omega-6 fatty acids and our body needs this balance. Omega-3s have been shown to reduce inflammation and be protective against cancer, while too much Omega-6 fats cause inflammation and increase cancer risk.

Over time, consumption of these oils high in Omega-6s and polyunsaturated fats can also lead to other problems.The journal Epidemiology published a study called, "Margarine Intake and Subsequent Coronary Heart Disease in Men." Authors of the study followed participants of the Framingham Heart Study for 20 years and recorded their incidence of heart attack. They also tracked both butter and margarine consumption.

The researchers discovered that as margarine consumption increased... heart attacks went up. As butter consumption increased... heart attacks declined.

The study also divided the data into ten-year increments. What they discovered is that during the first ten years, there was little association between margarine consumption and heart attacks. However, during the second decade of follow-up, the group eating the most margarine had 77% more heart attacks than the group eating none!

Imbalance of these fats can also cause damage to the intestines and along with processed grain consumption can set the body up for a host of food allergies and auto-immune problems. (This was likely at least partially the cause of my own autoimmune disease.)

reproductive problems and problems in children caused by vegetable oil consumption

Vegetable oils are extremely damaging to the reproductive system and the developing bodies of unborn babies and children. Because the reproductive system in both men and women is constantly producing and dividing new cells, there is high potential for mutation and problems when these cells are made of the wrong kind of fats and are oxidized.

This same thing applies to unborn babies and children, whose cells are dividing at high rates. There is more potential for mutation because there are more cells dividing.

Science does tell us that low fat diets in babies and children, or diets where vegetable oils have been completely substituted for animal based fats can result in failure to thrive as well as developmental delays. These types of diets can also lead to hormonal problems and infertility. Teenage girls who adhere to such a diet risk reproductive problems. If they do manage to conceive, their chances of giving birth to a low birth weight baby, or a baby with birth defects, are high.

Excess consumption of vegetable oils also causes problems with hormone production, since hormones are dependent on certain fats for their manufacture. Vegetable oils that are hardened by hydrogenation to make shortening or margarine are especially damaging.

other effects of vegetable oils on the body

Because vegetable oils oxidize easily, they also deplete the body of antioxidants since the body must use these to attempt to neutralize the oxidation. People with high consumption of vegetable oils and their products are at risk for Vitamin E deficiency and other deficiencies.

In animal studies, diets high in polyunsaturates from vegetable oils made it difficult for subjects to learn (especially if they were exposed to stress). Animals exhibited decreased immune function and increased rates of disease. Vegetable oils depressed the mental and physical growth of infants; increased levels of uric acid in the blood and cause abnormal fatty acid profiles in the fat tissues. They have been linked to mental decline and chromosomal damage and they accelerate aging. Excessive consumption of polyunsaturates is associated with increasing rates of cancer, heart disease and weight gain.

In light of all that information, how do you sort out which oils are healthy, and which ones aren't? Even more important, how do you know how much of each one to consume to be healthy?

oils and fats to avoid:

Vegetable Oils and their fats should be avoided completely. There are much healthier alternatives and there is no reason or need to consume these types of fats. The main culprits to watch out for are:

- Canola Oil
- Corn Oil
- Soybean Oil
- "Vegetable" Oil
- Peanut Oil
- Sunflower Oil
- Safflower Oil
- Cottonseed Oil
- Grapeseed Oil

- Margarine
- Shortening
- I Can't Believe It's Not Butter® (You better believe it!)
- Smart Balance® (Not a smart idea!)
- Any other fake butter or vegetable oil products

While it is simple enough to avoid these oils themselves, the tougher challenge is avoiding all the foods they are in. Check out practically any processed food, and you will find at least one of these ingredients, often labeled as "partially hydrogenated corn/soybean/etc. oil" or "May contain soybean or canola oil." These foods in particular often contain one of the above unhealthy oils:

- Salad Dressings
- Store Bought Condiments
- Mayo
- Chips
- Artificial Cheeses
- Store-bought Nuts and Snacks

- Cookies
- Crackers
- Snack Foods
- Sauces
- Practically anything sold in the middle aisles of the store

oils and fats to use freely:

There are so many wonderful and healthy fats that are beneficial to the body, so there is no reason to consume the unhealthy ones above. Fats that can be consumed freely for optimal health are:

Coconut Oil: Filled with Medium Chain Fatty Acids and Lauric Acid, coconut oil is an all-star of the saturated fats. Since the fat composition in cells in the body is largely saturated fat, it is important to get enough of it from healthy sources. Coconut oil does not oxidize easily at high temperatures or go rancid easily, making it a good choice for cooking and baking. It can be substituted for butter and also makes a great natural moisturizer.

Meats: Meat, especially red meat, has gotten a bad rap. Unfortunately, the animals we eat have been as mistreated nutritionally as we have. Meats like grass-fed beef and free-range chicken have a very different nutritional profile than their feedlot counterparts. Grass-fed and free-range meats have higher nutrient levels, healthy forms of saturated fats and even Omega-3s. If possible, consume these forms of meat.

Butter: This is the one food people are happiest to start using again. Butter tastes delicious, and pastured, grass-fed butter is an excellent source of fat soluble vitamins, healthy saturated fat and other nutrients. It contains a compound that Weston A. Price called Activator X, known to improve nutrient absorption and have preventative benefits against disease.

Organic Cream: Also a good source of healthy saturated fat, organic heavy cream is essentially liquid butter, and is great served whipped on top of fruit, in desserts or in cream based recipes.

Olive Oil: High in monounsaturated fats (and low in polyunsaturated fats), olive oil is a great oil for salad dressings, homemade mayo, and cold recipes. It shouldn't be used for cooking since its high monounsaturated fat content makes it susceptible to oxidation at high temperatures.

Palm Oil: Has a high saturated fat content and is also heat stable. Some sources claim that palm oil production often encroaches on the natural habitat of some endangered animals, though sustainable versions can be found. If in doubt, just use coconut oil.

Avocados and Avocado Oil: A good source of monounsaturated fats and great on salads or in guacamole. Avocado oil is milky-tasting and can be used in salad dressings.

Fish: Fish are naturally high in Omega-3 fatty acids and can help improve the Omega-3/Omega-6 balance in the body. Look for sustainable wild caught sources, and stick to small fish like tuna, sardines, salmon, etc. to minimize mercury.

Eggs: Another all-star in the healthy fats community, eggs are loaded with vitamins, healthy fats, and necessary cholesterol. Consume them daily from free-range sources.

oils and fats to consume in moderation:

Some fats are nutritious and beneficial to the body but should still be consumed in moderation if they are eaten. Many contain high levels of Omega-6 fats and can therefore mess up the balance of fats in the body.

Flaxseed Oil: Though it contains a good amount of Omega-3s, it also has a lot of Omega-6s and its high Polyunsaturated fat content makes it prone to oxidation if heated. Fish oil is a much better source of Omega-3s, and in general, I don't recommend flax oil, though it certainly is not the worst option.

Walnut Oil: Also high in Omega-6 fats, but it has a great rich taste and can be safely used occasionally in dressings or desserts. It also has a slightly higher resistance to oxidation at higher temperatures than other nut oils.

Macadamia Nut Oil: This is one of my favorite tasting oils, but it is expensive. It is great in salad dressings or mayo. It has a lot of monounsaturated fats and low levels of polyunsaturated fats.

Nuts: Most types of nuts (remember peanuts are not nuts) are a good source of protein and healthy fats and can be eaten in moderation without problem. Just check to make sure they haven't been cooked in vegetable oils, which is often the case. Nuts also contain phytic acid, so consuming them in excess can be problematic for tooth and bone health.

the not-so-sweet truth about sugar

"This may seem exaggerated and far-fetched, but sugar is the most dangerous drug of the times and can still be easily acquired everywhere."

- Paul van der Velpen, the head of Amsterdam's health service

All things in moderation....

A little bit won't hurt...

It's fuel for the brain...

All justifications for consuming sugar in some amount. The question is: should sugar ever be consumed and if so, in what amount?

the problem with sugar:

Sugar exists in many forms besides just the white powdered (usually GMO) beet sugar we can pick up at the grocery store. Sugar in all of its forms (including corn syrup, honey, and maple syrup) affects the body in a powerful way and we are consuming more of it now than ever before. For instance:

Consumption of processed foods and sugar cost the American people over $50 billion a year in dental bills. Our nation is addicted to sugar and consuming more than ever before. In 1915, the average person consumed 15-20 pounds of sugar per year.

Recent statistics show that the average person consumes his or her weight in sugar per year plus up to 20 pounds of corn syrup or processed sweeteners or alternatives. This drastic change in sugar consumption in such a short period of time has created some not-so-sweet consequences for our health.

I often hear the argument that sugar is ok in moderation and that eliminating any "food group" is dangerous. Certainly, avoiding an actual macronutrient category completely (carbohydrate, protein or fat) would be problematic, but sugar itself is not a food group. Though sugar in some form is naturally present in many foods, by itself, it contains:

- no nutrients
- no protein
- no healthy fats
- no enzymes

Really, sugar is just empty and quickly digested calories. Further, it can actually pull minerals from the body during digestion and create a hormone cascade that starts a positive feedback loop in the body to encourage more consumption. In a time when famine was common, and we needed to consume large amounts in the summer while there was any food available in order to survive the winter scarcity, this was a good thing. In today's world of constant access to sugary foods, it is not so helpful.

what's in sugar?

Most often, when we talk about sugar, we are referring to a mixture of glucose and fructose, both simple sugars that are contained in various amounts in different foods. There are now dozens of sugar variations and artificial sweeteners in the standard diet today:

- Simple sugars (monosaccharides): Dextrose, fructose, and glucose.
- Complex Sugars (Disaccharides): Combinations of simple sugars like fructose and glucose.
- High fructose corn syrup (HFCS) is 55 percent fructose and 45 percent glucose.
- Sugar alcohols like xylitol, glycerol, sorbitol, maltitol, mannitol, and erythritol are technically neither sugars nor alcohols but are becoming increasingly popular as sweeteners. They are not easily absorbed by the small intestine so they provide fewer calories than sugar but often cause problems with bloating, diarrhea, and flatulence.
- Sucralose (the ingredient in Splenda) is NOT a sugar. It is a chlorinated artificial sweetener similar to aspartame and saccharin, with detrimental health effects to match.

- Agave syrup is a processed sweetener that is usually 80 percent fructose. The end product does not even remotely resemble the original agave plant.
- Honey is about half fructose but is completely natural in its raw form and has many health benefits, like as many antioxidants as spinach, when used in moderation,.
- Stevia is a highly sweet herb derived from the leaf of the South American stevia plant, which is completely safe (in its natural form).

is there any safe amount?

In my opinion, there is no safe amount of added sugar. Naturally contained sugars in fruit and vegetables are balanced by the fiber, vitamins, enzymes and other properties of the fruit/vegetable, which slow sugar digestion and help the body deal with it more easily. Added sugar, on the other hand, provides none of these benefits and instead:

- Stresses the Liver: When we consume fructose, it goes to the liver. If liver glycogen is low, such as after exercise, the body will use the fructose to replenish liver glycogen. Most people aren't consuming fructose only after a long workout and their livers are already full of glycogen. If fructose is consumed when the liver already has adequate glycogen and the body has an excess of fructose, the liver turns the fructose in to fat to store it. Some of this fat is sent to the cells for storage but some can remain in the liver. This is the condition referred to as Non-Alcoholic Fatty Liver Disease.
- Increases Bad Cholesterol and Triglycerides
- Can contribute to Leptin Resistance (and then weight gain, cravings, sleep trouble, etc)
- Creates an addictive sugar response in the brain
- Doesn't fill you up and instead encourages you to eat more

practically speaking...

I realize that in today's world, it can be tough to completely avoid sugar since it is so readily available. Unfortunately, the widespread availability of sugar doesn't make it any healthier...

Especially for kids who are still developing their nutritional foundation, metabolism, and hormones, even a little sugar can be harmful. As hard as it can be sometimes, we try to stick to whole, real foods as much as possible and avoid any processed foods (especially those containing grains and sugars.)

For us, this means cooking at home almost all the time. We work to teach our children about healthy eating at home, but I also don't completely restrict unhealthy foods if we are away from home for a few reasons...

While they are young now and it is easy to make sure they are eating healthy foods, especially at home, they will one day grow up and be away from home and exposed to all types of foods. I think it is important to let them start to make food choices on their own (and they usually make healthy ones) while they are still young and I can still help guide their choices rather than completely restrict them.

When kids are used to eating a really healthy diet, even a small amount of processed food will usually make them feel "yucky" and discourage them from eating it again.

Exposure to other foods often leads to conversations about different types of foods and which are good/bad for the body.

My kids typically make good food choices on their own and have become rather adventurous eaters since they aren't restricted or expected to only consume chicken fingers or hamburgers when we aren't at home. For instance, my two year old loves broccoli, olives, sardines and other healthy foods. Make the good foods readily available and make the unhealthy ones few and far between.

We also don't consume sugary drinks – even juice. The only reason we keep sugar around is for making Kombucha, water kefir, and homemade sodas. In these drinks, the great majority of the sugar is fermented out and converted to beneficial bacteria before we drink it.

Our breakfasts usually consist of eggs or leftovers, lunches are salads or soups and dinners are often baked or grilled meat with lots of veggies.

Sounds like a lot of work? It certainly is more work than a meal-in-a-box meal, but so worth it! We haven't had to take any of the kids to the doctor in years for illnesses, all but one have never had antibiotics and they are happily active and fit naturally. My hope as they grow is to nurture their own healthy eating habits and develop a lifelong foundation for healthy eating.

making real food work for your family

"Family is not an important thing. It's everything."

- Michael J. Fox

Keeping a well-stocked kitchen is essential for sticking to a real food lifestyle. If you've got healthy foods at your fingertips all the time and no processed foods to fall back on, you won't be tempted to reach for the cereal on a busy morning.

For me, keeping a kitchen stocked and meal planning have been the two biggest factors that keep our family eating real foods!

stocking a real food pantry

When you must keep large amounts of non-perishables on hand, buying them in bulk when they are on sale is a great way to save money. I have really limited pantry space, so instead of all my non-perishables being in one big closet, they are spread out all over my kitchen. Luckily, I cook with a lot of fresh or frozen ingredients, so they don't compete for space.

These are the foods I keep in my pantry at all times:

Coconut Products: Coconut oil, shredded coconut, coconut flour, coconut cream, etc. We go through these things quickly. In addition to being staples of many of my recipes, they make great snacks! Look for unrefined, organic, cold pressed versions.

Olive Oil: Great for making salad dressings and adding to foods once they are cooked. It is a great source of monounsaturated fats. Just don't use it for cooking or it can oxidize!

Other Fats and Oils: Lard, Tallow and Ghee: I either make or order these in big quantities and store in 1 or 5 gallon bucketsto have around for cooking.

Vinegars: White Vinegar for cleaning, other vinegars like balsamic and apple cider for cooking. I also use apple cider/balsamic/red wine for salad dressings and marinades and drink a couple tablespoons of Apple Cider Vinegar in water if I feel a cold coming on.

Nuts: Walnuts, cashews, almonds, macadamia nuts etc. are great for on-the-go snacks. If I can, I soak and then dehydrate these before storing to reduce the phytic acid. (P.S. Macadamia nuts that have been dipped in 90% dark chocolate and then cooled are one of my favorite treats)

Canned Fish: Canned fish (though not the perfect choice), is a way to pack protein on the go, or a fast meal in a pinch. I keep sardines, tuna, wild caught salmon, etc. on hand to make tuna salads, salmon patties, etc. There are even organic sustainable tuna options.

Self Canned Veggies: I've been canning most of my own veggies and sauces to reduce our BPA exposure. Many store-bought canned vegetables, and all tomatoes (as far as I know) have a BPA lining in the can. It is certainly time consuming, but I make ketchup, tomato sauce, tomato paste, diced tomatoes, hot sauce, tomato soup, etc. from the tomatoes in our garden. If you don't have this option, look for these foods in glass jars, not cans!

Vegetables: Vegetables that don't need to be refrigerated can keep in the pantry for a long time. We keep sweet potatoes, onions, winter squash, garlic, etc. on hand in the pantry and they always get eaten before they spoil.

Herbs and Spices: I have an entire cabinet stocked with nothing but medicinal and culinary herbs and spices. In my opinion, the right high-quality spices can make the difference between a good meal and a great one. I also use my herbs to make iced herbal teas, tinctures, and for medicinal use if one of us gets sick.

I usually have on hand:

Culinary Uses:

- Basil
- Thyme
- Oregano
- Rosemary
- Garlic (powder, granules, minced, salt)
- Turmeric
- Cayenne
- Cinnamon
- Sea Salt (Himalayan, Black Lava, Smoked)
- Cumin
- Chili Powder
- Celery Salt
- Savory
- Dill
- Onion Powder and Salt
- Mint
- Bay Leaf
- Caraway
- Cardamon
- Marjoram
- Parsley
- Pepper

Medicinal/tea:

- Alfalfa
- Nettle
- Dandelion
- Peppermint
- Spearmint
- Red Raspberry Leaf
- Chamomile
- Ginger
- Activated Charcoal
- Elderberries
- Bilberry
- Black Walnut
- Calendula
- Catnip
- Coltsfoot
- Echinacea
- Fennel
- Fenugreek
- Ginko
- Ginseng
- Goldenseal
- Hops
- Horsetail
- Lavender
- Lemon Balm
- Licorice
- Oatstraw
- Red Clover
- Spurlina
- Stevia Leaf
- Kelp

Check out my homemade spice blends on page 260 and some homemade herbal tea recipes on page 318.

baking ingredients

Almond flour, baking powder (aluminum free), baking soda, cocoa powder, vanilla, almond butter, dark baking chocolate, etc.

stocking a real food fridge

The fridge is harder to keep stocked, at least around here. As fast as my kids go through eggs, bacon, apples, and cucumbers, it never seems to stay full!

These are the things I always (try) to keep stocked in my fridge:

Vegetables: Sliced cucumbers, carrots and celery are on hand for snacks. I also keep lots of lettuce and spinach for salads. Cabbage sauerkraut is usually in some stage of fermentation on my counter. To mix things up, I try to also keep artichokes, leeks, peppers, tomatoes, avocados, cauliflower, broccoli, greens, squashes etc. on hand.

Fruits: We try to stick with seasonal fruit, but I usually keep apples and oranges around for the kids. If they are in season, we usually have citrus fruits. If not, I just keep lemon and lime juice for adding to water.

Coconut Milk: There is always at least a gallon of homemade or store-bought coconut milk in the fridge for smoothies and drinks for the kids.

Yogurt: Though we don't eat much yogurt, I keep the full fat organic kind on hand to separate into whey for fermenting and cream cheese for cooking and veggie dips.

Meats: These are kept in the fridge or freezer and I usually don't keep more than a day or two's worth of meat defrosted at once.

Eggs: We go through at least a dozen eggs a day, so keeping these around is tough. If I can stay on top of it, I try to keep 5-6 dozen cartons in the fridge, including at least a dozen already boiled ones for snacks.

Condiments: I've resorted to making most of my own, but the following condiments are usually in the fridge: mustard, homemade mayo, homemade ketchup, homemade tomato sauce, homemade hot sauce, apple cider vinegar, lemon juice, lime juice, chlorophyll, homemade pickles and relish, etc. See recipes for these on page 238.

other places we keep/store food

To be able to purchase in bulk, we have a stand-up deep freezer and an extra fridge in our shed. We also keep a garden. The deep freezer is full of a quarter of a cow that we purchased from a local farmer, and some frozen veggies from last year's garden. I also really stock up on nitrite-free bacon, sausage, and hot dogs when they are on sale.

During the summer months, most of our vegetables come from the garden, which helps the food budget a lot!

meal planning

"All great change in America
begins at the dinner table."

- Ronald Reagan

Meal Planning makes a big difference when it comes to sticking to a
dietary change. It's easy to cook a quick convenience food or head to a
restaurant when everyone is hungry and nothing is defrosted, but a little
planning can prevent this! If you have kids, you can involve them in the
planning as well, which will help them get excited about (and willing to
try) the healthy foods you are cooking

Here are seven tips to help you plan out weekly meals for your family:

1. Have A Daily Template

Rather than starting from scratch each week, I have a template of the general types of foods I cook each day of the week and the number of times I use each main food. For example, each week I cook:

- 1-2 stir frys
- 1 salad
- 1 slow cooker or soup meal
- 1 fish/seafood meal
- 1-2 prepare ahead oven meals

I try to use no meat more than twice so in a given week I might have 2 beef meals, 2 chicken meals, 1 fish meal and 2 pork or egg meals.

2. Focus On Core Recipes

As you find recipes your family enjoys, make them core recipes that get re-used every few weeks. Try to build up about 20 of these and you won't ever be bored with your meals. Each week, use these core meals for 5 of your dinners and try something new for 2 dinners. If you get really motivated, build 20 core meals for each season: find favorite dishes that use seasonal produce and rotate with the seasons. This will also save money on produce.

3. Stretch Your Protein

Protein is typically the most expensive part of the meal so if you can use less expensive cuts of meat and stretch them, it might allow you to buy organic and grass-fed rather than conventional meats. This is another reason I love stir frys and casseroles: you can add more veggies and stretch the meat more than if you were just serving baked chicken alone. The slow cooker is a great way to make tougher, cheaper cuts of meat tender.

4. Mix it up with Spices

A basic easy recipe (like Chicken Squash Stir Fry or Pakistani Kima) can taste completely different just by changing the spices. Add some cumin and chili powder and you have a Mexican flavor, or some Curry for an Indian flavor. Basil, thyme, oregano, and garlic give an Italian flavor while Chinese 5 Spice gives an Asian flair. I buy all my herbs from Mountain Rose Herbs in bulk since it saves money and I've found that the herbs and spices are very high quality.

5. Travel the World In Your Kitchen

One of my dreams is to travel the world and try the different cuisines in each country. Since that isn't possible right now, I try to create the same experience in my kitchen. With a little research and some healthy adjustments, you can recreate recipes from around the world. You might be surprised to find that your kids enjoy the flavors of Indian or Thai food or that you have a passion for French flavors.

6. Don't Be A Short Order Cook

Want to raise a picky eater? Let your child eat whatever he/she wants and cater to his or her food preferences. Want to not raise a picky eater? Expose your children to healthy and diverse foods from a young age and don't make any specific foods for them. My one year old gladly eats curries, cooked vegetables, liver, and avocado because she's never had crackers, toast, chicken nuggets, or juice.

Not only is this more nutritious for kids, but it will really be a benefit to them in the long run.

Check out our "food rules to cure picky eating" on page 43.

7. Eat Leftovers for Breakfast and Lunch

It can be tough to break the cereal-and-sandwich mindset but an easy, time-saving way to eat healthy is to make extra food and serve the same meals again for breakfast and lunch. Most foods (except soups) can also be added to an omelet for breakfast or put with a salad for lunch. Cold meatza or barbecue, for example, makes a delicious breakfast or lunch.

Another easy trick is to make salads or store leftovers in mason jars (liquid ingredients at the bottom for salads, then meat/toppings, then lettuce) and store in the fridge. Then, the meal can be re-heated easily or dumped onto a plate to serve.

10 tips for real food on a budget

"Tell me what you eat, and I will tell you what you are."

- Anthelme Brillat Savarin

Tip #1: Most Important Factor In Eating Healthy Without Breaking the Bank- Meal Planning!

This alone has made the biggest difference in reducing our food budget and staying on track to eat healthy foods. Meal planning allows me to make some foods ahead and have them available for lunches or to re-purpose for dinners.

Since I started meal planning, I am also able to go to the store only once a week or less and can often prepare most of the food for the week in one day, which cuts down my overall food prep time.

The system I use for meal planning and rotating meals is simple to adapt using your own favorite foods and dishes. The meal plans below let us eat a different meal each night of the month and then repeat. I also have more seasonal plans for Summer and Fall.

To make your own healthy meal plan system:

Write down 14-28 healthy recipes that your family likes. If your budget is tight, pick recipes that are also inexpensive to make.
On the front of a 3×5 index card, write the meal and the recipe.
On the back of the index card, write how much of each ingredient is needed for this recipe for your family size. (I usually plan for leftovers for lunches)

To meal plan: once a week or once a month, pick out the number of meals you need and put them in order for the week.

Bonus: turn them over, add up the total of the ingredients, and you have a shopping list (just cross off any ingredients you have already)!

Stick the cards on the fridge or bulletin board and put them away in your recipe box as you use them.

By making you stick to a list, this system helps ensure that you always have foods prepared or ready to prepare, limiting impulsive purchasing and eating. On busy nights or when we are in a rush, stir frys are my go-to dinner. Just throw some leftover meat and a few bags of frozen veggies in a skillet or wok with some butter, and viola- dinner in minutes!

Tip # 2- Prepare in Bulk

I've found this especially helpful with regards to meat. When our budget is tightest, I prepare a large, inexpensive cut of meat and reuse it different ways throughout the week. I always keep an eye out for items like Turkey, Ham, Brisket, etc. to go on sale for these occasions.

A couple of weeks ago, for instance, I found whole turkeys on sale for 39 cents a pound, which worked out to between $5 and $6 per turkey... I bought seven. Now, when we have company, (or even when we don't) I just stick a turkey in the oven and have leftovers for the whole week.

To further stretch the budget, use the bones of any meat you eat to make a healthy bone broth or stock. Both can be stored in the freezer or even canned (make sure you follow instructions carefully when using any kind of meat product) to stretch them even further.

Some examples of how to repurpose the meats:

- For turkey: leftover meat rolled in lettuce leaves for lunches, made into turkey enchiladas for dinners, slow-cooked in Crock Pot for soups, added to omelets, put in stir frys etc. Bones used for broth/ stock.
- For beef (brisket, roast, etc.): leftover meat is seasoned for fajitas, put in omelets, made into barbecue, thrown in soups, made into omelet quesadillas, etc. Bones used for broth/stock.
- For ham: roasted with cauliflower for "ham and potatoes" dish, used with bone for ham bone soup, put in omelets, wrapped up in lettuce or on salads for lunch, stir fry with cabbage for fast meal, etc.
- You can also prepare large amounts of ground beef, chicken breasts or any other meat you have around and structure your meals for the week around this.

Tip #3- Find Inexpensive Vegetables

Veggies can vary tremendously in price, depending on the time of year and the source. Focusing on veggies that are in season will help cut costs some.

In the winter, we use a lot of frozen vegetables since they are cheaper, and in my opinion, frequently fresher than the "fresh" produce that has been shipped halfway around the world.

Vegetables like cabbage and sweet potatoes are inexpensive year round and can be great fillers and substitutes in recipes. I stock up on things like these when they are in season, usually buying several cases of sweet potatoes in the fall from farmers markets.

Cabbage costs just pennies a pound from farmers when in season, and can be made into sauerkraut for later use.

Winter squash also stores well and we buy this in bulk too.

Farmers markets, CSAs, and local farmers are great resources for buying inexpensive veggies in bulk. (more on that below)

Tip #4- Order in Bulk

Though there is more of a cost upfront, ordering in bulk can usually save money in the long run. We order non-perishables like coconut flour, shredded coconut, olive oil, coconut oil, herbal teas, liquid castille soap, almond flour, etc. in bulk from a co-op.

We also order cheese in bulk 10-20 pound blocks at a time from an organic farmer who offers raw cheese. Finding these resources in your area can be tricky, but once you establish a relationship with farmers, it can be a tremendous help to the budget.

Tip # 5- Find a CSA, Farmer's Market or Local Farmer

Websites like LocalHarvest.com and EatWellGuide.com can help you find a farmer, CSA (Community Supported Agriculture), or farmers market in your area. Websites like EatWild.com have resources for finding a local supplier of grassfed beef or other healthy animals.

Ask around too! We get most of our meats and vegetables from Amish farmers, but they don't have listings online. Check with local health food stores- many will know places to find these items locally.

Tip # 6- Grow Your Own Food

Even if you live in a big city, it is often possible to grow at least some of your own food. We have a 25 x 40 foot garden for vegetables, and also have fruit trees, grape vines and blueberry bushes in the works this year.

We are able to grow enough vegetables for summer, with excess that we preserve throughout the year, for our family of 7 in this space. We offset a lot of our food bill last year by growing our own, and it was much easier than I expected.

I haven't tried it myself, but a lot of people recommend Square Foot Gardening to maximize space in small yards. Consider checking out a book on this if you are tight on space.

Tip # 7- Get Some Chickens and Even a Cow!

If your means allow, having chickens is also a great way to save money and have a great sustainable protein source. Websites like backyardchickens.com offer a lot of information about raising chickens, even in a small backyard.

For most people it isn't feasible, but having a cow can also really cut down on the food bill in the long run. Right now, we get our beef from cow-sharing, where we purchase part of a live cow and pick up the meat once it is processed. If keeping a cow isn't for you, look for a farmer that offers grass-fed beef in your area.

Tip # 8- Preserve When Possible

Another factor that can really help cut down a food bill is the ability to preserve foods for use when they aren't in season. Last year I tried my hand at canning, and we are still enjoying the outcome.

This year, the goal is to can all of our tomato products for the year to cut down on BPA exposure from canned tomatoes. I also plan to can applesauce by buying several bushels when apples are in season and making our own. Last year, we also canned condiments and pickles, and will do this again.

Freezing is another way to preserve foods, and our extra deep freeze in our shed has been a tremendous help for storing our 1/4 of beef and veggies from the garden.

Dehydrating is another option, though it takes a while and can be a slow process, at least with my dehydrator. If money is tight, look for dehydrators and canners at garage sales and thrift stores to save money, rather than buying new.

Tip # 9- Don't Buy Drinks!

If you are trying to eat healthy, hopefully you've already cut out things like soda, canned drinks, and processed juices from your food budget. If not, do it now! This alone is a big step in improving overall health.

If you have consumed much of these beverages in the past, go back and look at the percentage of your food bill that they take up. In general, buying beverages in any prepared form is an expensive and unhealthy option.

Even fruit juices cause a big insulin spike in the body, and are expensive without offering much nutrition. Pasteurized milk isn't a healthy option either: it contains some levels or hormones, and the nutrients have been largely removed by the pasteurization process.

Cutting those items from the grocery budget will often free up a lot of cash for healthier options. If you aren't a fan of only drinking water, ever... there are still some healthier and cheaper options for nutritious drinks.

Tip # 10- Save Money in Other Areas

The biggest advantage to eating a healthy real food diet is saving money in other areas (like doctor bills!). We haven't been to a doctor for illnesses since we started eating this way all the time, and we all coast through flu season without a problem.

There are other areas of a budget where you can save money to help buffer the food bill also. Here are some of the way's we've done it:

- We don't eat out... ever. I admit it: I love eating out. Not because the food is good (it usually isn't) but because it means that I don't have to cook or clean for one whole meal. This is a big deal when you cook three hot meals a day and then have to do the dishes (and mop the floor as the case may be with a one year old!). That being said, eating out even once a month can use up a lot of the food budget at once. Saving the money from eating out lets me provide healthier options for my family at home, and none of us miss eating out that much.

- Make expensive baby items at home: I've saved money by making my own Natural Homemade Baby Wipes, baby food, and cloth diapers. All of these items are expensive in stores and healthier when made at home.

- Make Your Own Natural Cosmetics/Beauty Products- This is another area to save money and get healthier options. Try using some natural homemade substitutes for conventional beauty products or making your own deodorant and toothpaste.

- Make Your Own Cleaning Products- This one is so easy and saves a lot of money. If you aren't doing this already, you should be, and you probably already have the stuff at home. White vinegar, baking soda, washing soda and natural soap are often all you need to keep your home clean naturally and inexpensively.

- Cut Back on Supplements- Unless you are taking a very specific supplement for a condition, chances are you can back off of some supplements when you start eating healthier. You can also get vitamins, minerals and probiotics much more inexpensively by making herbal teas, bone broths, and kefir/kombucha. Your diet is naturally higher in these things too, so if you have to cut back on the supplements to eat a real food diet, consider it a fair trade. Supplements are meant to "supplement" a good diet anyway, and it's really impossible to out-supplement a bad diet. In general, it is better to have healthy food options than to pop pills.

- Exercise at Home or With Your Kids- Chances are you already have running shoes (or not: the barefoot exercising trend is growing, and for good reason). If you are paying for a gym membership, consider using this money for real food instead. Do some sprints outside or learn how to do proper pushups at home. Make exercise fun without being a gym-rat by playing a game of soccer with the kids. Added bonus: you are keeping your kids active too!

- Do a Media Detox: If you've made the above changes and money is still tight, consider doing a media "detox"by cutting back on entertainment related expenses. We cut out cable a couple years ago, and we don't even miss it. Face it- the news is usually depressing and it doesn't seem to be getting much better. Consider getting rid of the cable, newspaper subscription, new radio, etc. to have money to put in healthier areas of your life. Our kids don't get video-games either (oh, the horror!) and they don't care... they have this great entertainment system called the backyard!

food rules to cure picky eating

"The only real stumbling block
is fear of failure. In cooking
you've got to have a
what-the-hell attitude."

- Julia Child

Many parents assume that kids won't eat or won't like certain foods, even if the children themselves have never complained: in other words, parents assume kids are picky eaters from the start, without any evidence.

There is a perception that foods like chicken nuggets, sandwiches and pre-packaged kid-sized snacks are the foods of choice for kids, and we parents are hesitant to introduce foods that we fear they won't like. Unfortunately, by doing this we create the picky eaters we fear we already have.

I've also found that the attitude we teach about food is as important as the food choices we offer. In the times I've visited other countries, there is a difference in how children ask for, eat, and behave in food related situations.

While I certainly think that the types of foods we market to and prepare for our children needs to change, I think it is also important to change the way our kids think about food as well.

To this end, I pulled some ideas from my mom's French background (after noticing that her family was naturally thin, not picky and ate a wide variety of foods). We've incorporated these ideas with our own children, and the difference has been astounding.

I call these "Food Rules" though the name is slightly misleading. I think that while we certainly must have guidelines about how children act in food related situations, these "rules" should be taught by example and practice rather than iron fist (or wooden spoon).

1. No Complaining About Food

In our house, children (and adults) are not allowed to complain about food. This doesn't mean that they are forced to eat at every meal, just that negative talk about food is not permitted.

Food is first for nourishment, not for taste, appearance, etc., and this is an important thing to teach children. Additionally, complaining about food is both rude to the cook and shows a closed-minded attitude.

How we handle it: No one is ever forced to eat if truly not hungry but everyone must sit and participate in meal times with a positive attitude. Those who insist on a negative attitude are dismissed for bedtime. Especially with multiple kids, a negative mentality about a certain food spreads quickly and is hard to counteract, so it is better to head this off thoroughly!

2. Food is not a Reward

Food is, again, first provided for nourishment, not entertainment or emotional reward. For this reason, we try (not always perfectly) not to bribe with food or offer food as rewards for good behavior. I even try not to make certain foods a big deal on birthdays or other occasions, as we try to focus on experiences instead. (i.e. instead of a birthday cake and sugary snacks, we might take a family trip to the zoo or other fun place for a birthday).

In the same way, I don't ever present foods as a punishment or associate them with punishment (i.e. "You have to eat your asparagus or you are getting spanked.") While children can't complain about food, it is the negative attitude that is disciplined, not the action relating to food.

I've seen in many children (and even to some degree in myself at times) an emotional connection to a certain food, or a desire to eat certain foods in emotional situations. While the types of foods we provide is certainly important, it is also important to avoid creating an association between foods (especially unhealthy ones) and happy times or fond memories. I'd personally much rather those fond memories be connected to family time and experiences anyway!

How we handle it: While we do, of course, sometimes have treats, they are just given when I make them. We don't use them as a bribe, kids don't earn them through good behavior or good grades, and we don't withhold them if children misbehave.

3. Eating is a Family Activity:

I think that the trend of eating on-the-go and in isolation (while watching TV, etc) has contributed a lot to the negative attitudes children have about food. For this reason, we make a sincere effort to eat meals (especially breakfast and dinner) as a family when at all possible and to make this an enjoyable time.

The advantages are that meal times (hopefully) provide an enjoyable time for conversation and bonding with the children, which also facilitates slower and more mindful eating.
In our house, the whole family also eats the same thing at each meal. Children don't get special kid-friendly foods and as soon as little ones can eat solids, they get tiny pieces of what the rest of us are eating. The family atmosphere helps encourage children to eat what is served, and helps us parents avoid food battles.

If a food is unusual or a new food for us, we don't make a big deal about it (by not saying anything about it) and just present it to the kids with a positive attitude and assume that they will eat it. I've seen my husband choke down liver with a poker face (poor guy!) and the kids eat it readily because they have no idea that they shouldn't like it.

How we handle it: Meal time is family time and outside activities are rarely allowed to interfere. Everyone eats the same thing and eats it with a positive attitude (though if a person is truly not hungry, he or she may just sit there after tasting the food and enjoy the conversation). In the rare cases that children don't have a good attitude at meal times, they are excused to their rooms. We don't often snack, so everyone is ready to eat at meal times (though children do occasionally get healthy snacks if there will be longer than normal times between meals).

4. Try, Try Again

To help facilitate a non-picky palate in kids, they get one small bite of each food being served at a given meal (one green bean, one bite of sweet potatoes and a piece of chicken). When they finish one bite of each, they can request more of any food. When children don't like a food or request it when asking for more, we just explain that it is ok as long as they always are willing to try it and explain that one day (when they are grown up) they will like the food.

Dislike of foods is not set in stone so we don't force feed huge amounts of foods that they don't necessarily like. We just set the expectation that they will keep trying those foods until they do.

How we handle it: Just as negative comments about food are not allowed, we try to promote a positive attitude about new foods by presenting them in manageable (one bite) amounts accompanied by the expectation that they will learn to enjoy all foods one day.

5. Hunger is OK

I've worked with clients who have completely lost a natural sense of hunger due to constant access to foods and eating on-the-go. It is perfectly normal (and expected) to be hungry before meal times and hunger is never an excuse for negative attitudes about food or eating junk food.

Normal hunger at meal times encourages kids to eat what is served and to eat enough to avoid being hungry too far in advance of the next meal. At the same time, a child who complains and is excused from the dinner table for bedtime quickly learns to have a more positive attitude (it has never taken one of our kids more than two nights total of missing family dinner to find an improved attitude).

How we handle it: We don't let hunger be an excuse for unhealthy eating or bad attitudes. We don't often offer snacks frequently because children who are at least slightly hungry tend to be happier and more adventurous eaters at meal times.

6. Focus on Nutrient Dense Foods

Now for a few details on the actual types of foods we eat and why. I noticed that my mom (and the French in general) spend more time eating a smaller amount of high quality food. They enjoy it more and obsess about it less (in general). To help make all of the above "rules" easier to implement, I focus on cooking nutrient-dense, rich foods, from scratch each day. We incorporate bone broth, homemade pâté, raw cheeses, homemade sauces (that contain butter or cream), eggs and egg-based foods like hollandaise sauce on a daily basis.

Not only are omelets filled with meat and veggies and topped with hollandaise, but they are more nourished and have received a boost of beneficial fats (as opposed to what they get from a bowl of cereal). When possible, we let the kids help shop for or prepare the meals and I always make an effort to explain why certain types of food are more nutrient dense and how they benefit the body.

How we handle it: I cook from scratch every day, which is more time-consuming that throwing a sandwich together, but it is worth it to me to help my kids learn a healthy attitude toward food. You can check out my recipe index for some of the recipes we use.

"For each new morning
with its light,
For rest and shelter of the night,
For health and food,
for love and friends,
For everything Thy goodness sends."

- Ralph Waldo Emerson

Always buy organic	Ok to buy conventional
apples	asparagus
berries	avocado
celery	bananas
cherries	broccoli
cucumbers	cabbage
grapes	citrus fruits
kale	eggplant
lettuce	kiwi
peaches	mangos
pears	onions
peppers	peas
potatoes	pineapple
spinach	sweet potatoes
summer squash	watermelon
tomatoes	

breakfasts

"All happiness depends
on a leisurely breakfast."

- John Gunther

recipes

coconut flour MUFFINS
apple or banana

ingredients

- 5 eggs
- 1 cup homemade apple-sauce *(store bought should work too)*
- 1/2 cup coconut flour
- 2-3 tablespoons cinnamon
- 1 teaspoon baking soda
- 1 teaspoon vanilla *(optional)*
- 1/4 cup coconut oil
- 2 tablespoons honey *(optional)*

directions

1 Preheat the oven to 400 degrees F.

2 Grease a muffin pan with coconut oil.

3 Put all ingredients into a medium sized bowl and mix with immersion blender or whisk until well mixed.

4 Let sit 5 minutes.

5 Use 1/3 cup measure to spoon into muffin tins.

6 Bake 12-15 minutes until starting to brown and not soft when lightly touched on the top.

7 Let cool 2 minutes, drizzle with honey *(if desired)* and serve.

flavor options!

- Reduce the applesauce by 1/4 cup and add an overripe banana before blending. Mix in 1/2 cup toasted chopped nuts *(like walnuts)* by hand.
- Add 1/2 cup blueberries or raspberries
- Add 1/2 cup chopped apples for a little crunch
- Add 3 tablespoons of cocoa powder to make almost cupcake like

ingredients

- 1/3 cup nuts *(cashews, almonds, etc)* Reminder: peanuts are not nuts!
- 1/4 cup whole dates *(remove pits)* - about 3 large dates
- 1/4 cup raisins *(or more dates)*
- dash of cinnamon *(optional)*

directions

1. Put nuts into food processor *(or Vitamix)* and chop until in small pieces. Remove and put in bowl.

2. Put dates and raisins *(any combination of the two that equals 1/2 cup total)* into the food processor and pulse until playdough consistency. It will start to clump together when it is done.

3. Mix the two ingredients by hand until well incorporated and the consistency of stiff playdough or cookie dough. *(You can do this all in the food processor also)*

4. Roll between two sheets of wax paper to a 1/2 inch thickness and cut into bars. *(Or make it really easy and just roll into energy balls!)*

5. Wrap in wax paper, plastic wrap or snack size ziploc bags *(or glass containers if you aren't giving to kids)* and store in fridge until ready to use.

6. Enjoy!

chia seed ENERGY BARS

ingredients

- 6 large Medjool dates
- 1/2 cup chia seeds
- 2 tablespoons coconut oil
- Optional: 1/2 teaspoon natural vanilla extract or a pinch of cinnamon powder for taste
- Optional add ins: dark chocolate chips, shredded coconut, dried fruit (*a couple tablespoons of any add-in*)

directions

1. Remove the pits from the dates and pulse the dates in a food processor or blender until it forms a paste.

2. In a medium bowl, mix the date paste with the chia seeds and coconut oil. It will form a thick dough.

3. Roll this dough into balls or press into the bottom of a glass or silicon baking dish and cut into squares. It can be eaten immediately in dough-form. We prefer to put it in the fridge or freezer to give it more of a chewy texture. These can be wrapped in wax paper or parchment paper and sent for lunches or snacks.

grain free OATMEAL

ingredients

- a tablespoon of coconut oil
- a few eggs
- a couple tablespoons of almond butter
- a dash of vanilla
- a sprinkle of raisins
- dark chocolate *(totally optional)*

directions

1. Scramble eggs in the coconut oil until almost done but still somewhat soft.

2. Add all the other ingredients to taste and scramble until eggs are done cooking and ingredients are well mixed.

3. Eat while still warm... it is not good cold!

4. Enjoy... if you're in to weird things in your eggs!

coconut flour BISCUITS

ingredients

- 1/3 cup coconut flour
- 5 tablespoons butter or coconut oil, softened but not melted
- 4 eggs
- 2 tablespoons honey *(optional)*
- dash of salt
- 1/2 teaspoon baking powder

directions

1. Preheat oven to 400 degrees F.

2. Put all ingredients into medium sized bowl and mix well with immersion blender or hand mixer until well incorporated

3. Using your hands, carefully form into nine small balls and mash each one down with a spoon to make it about 1/2 inch thick.

4. Bake for 12-15 minutes until just starting to brown.

eggs BENEDICT

ingredients

- one batch (*10*) coconut flour biscuits (pg. 60)
- 10 eggs - cooked over medium
- 10 pieces of bacon (*preferably nitrite free*)
- hollandaise sauce (pg. 258)
- cheese (*optional*)

directions

1. Prepare the coconut flour biscuits and put into the oven.

2. Put bacon on a baking sheet and put into the oven also for about 10-12 minutes (*about the same amount of time as biscuits*)

3. While they are baking, make the hollandaise sauce. (*Note: if you can't eat dairy, you can use coconut oil or ghee in place of butter in the hollandaise sauce, though it does change the flavor*). Remove from heat and set aside.

4. In well oiled skillet, crack the eggs (*may have to do several batches*) being careful not to break the yolks. Cook just until yolks are barely set but still soft.

5. When biscuits are done, take out and put onto plates.

6. As eggs finish cooking, place one egg on top of each biscuit. Top with cheese if using.

7. Put one piece of bacon (*cut in half*) on top of each egg.

8. Top with a spoonful of Hollandaise sauce.

9. Serve immediately.

caprese OMELET

ingredients

- 2-4 eggs
- 2 tablespoons butter
- 1 small/medium tomato, diced
- 3-4 (*or more*) basil leaves, finely chopped
- shredded mozzarella to taste
- olive oil (*optional*)
- garlic, salt and pepper (*optional*)

directions

1 Melt butter in medium skillet over low/medium heat

2 Scramble eggs with fork in a shall bowl and season with garlic, salt and pepper if desired

3 Pour eggs into skillet and sprinkle tomatoes, cheese and basil on one half

4 When eggs are partially set, fold the empty half over to cover the side with tomatoes, basil and cheese

5 Cook until set, flipping if needed

6 Remove and promptly top with more tomatoes, basil and cheese and drizzle with olive oil if desired

coconut GRANOLA

ingredients

- 2 cups coconut chips
  (*I like these because they
  are bigger pieces*)

- 1 cup of nuts of choice
  (*I like a mix of cashews,
  sunflower seeds, pumpkin
  seeds and pecans*)

- 1/4 cup maple syrup

- 1/4 cup honey

- 1/4 cup coconut oil

- *optional:* vanilla
  (*1 teaspoon*), cinnamon
  (*dash*), chia seeds, raisins
  or other dried fruit of
  choice (*up to 1/2 cup*)

directions

1. Preheat the oven to 350 degrees F.

2. Melt coconut oil, honey and maple syrup in a small saucepan until starting to bubble and simmer.

3. Add vanilla if using.

4. In a large bowl, mix the coconut chips and nuts and any optional ingredients if using.

5. Pour honey/maple syrup/coconut oil mixture over the dry ingredients and mix well. The consistency will vary some depending on the honey, coconut chips, and coconut oil you use. If there is not enough of the honey mixture to lightly coat all of the ingredients, add slightly more melted coconut oil and honey in equal parts.

6. Spread on a parchment paper lined baking dish.

7. Bake for 15-20 until starting to brown.

8. Remove and let cool, then crumble in to granola pieces.

9. Store in an air tight jar and use within two weeks.

almond flour PANCAKES

ingredients

- 1.5 cups blanched almond flour

- 3 eggs

- 1 cup of water or milk (*or slightly less to desired thickness*)

- *Optional:* spices like cinnamon and nutmeg, vanilla, blueberries or other flavors

directions

1. Mix all ingredients in a medium sized bowl using a hand blender or immersion blender until batter is a pourable consistency.

2. Make one test pancake to check for desired thickness and texture.

3. Cook all pancakes on a griddle or in a large pan for approximately 2-3 minutes per side until bubble form and both sides are golden brown.

4. Enjoy!

sausage stuffed APPLES

ingredients

- 4-6 apples (*or 1 per person you are serving*)

- 1 pound sausage (*ground italian or breakfast sage, nitrate free*)

- 1 red onion, finely diced

- 2 tablespoons honey or maple syrup

- 1 large rib of celery, finely diced

- spices to taste: I used 1 teaspoon each of rosemary, thyme, sage, garlic powder, salt and pepper

directions

1. Preheat the oven to 375 degrees F.

2. Brown the sausage in a large skillet until completely cooked.

3. Remove sausage and add onion and celery to pan and saute until starting to soften.

4. Return sausage to pan, mix well and spice to taste.

5. Drizzle with the maple syrup or honey.

6. Cut each apple in half (*don't peel*) and scoop out the seed area with a spoon or sharp knife to make each apple a "bowl." Alternately, you can use a corer to remove most of the inside and leave the apples in tact (*as pictured*).

7. Spoon some of the sausage mixture into each apple and place on the bottom of a large baking dish.

8. Bake for 25-30 minutes until apples are cooked and fragrant.

9. Remove and serve with salad.

10. Enjoy!

ham and egg BREAKFAST CUPS

ingredients

- 12-24 pieces of nitrate free ham (*You can use 1 or 2 pieces per cup. Round slices work best.*)
- 12 eggs
- 2 green onions
- feta or other cheese to top (*optional*)

directions

1. Preheat the oven to 400 degrees F.
2. Line each compartment of a regular (12) muffin tin with 1 or 2 pieces of ham (*or other luncheon meat*)
3. Crack one egg into each compartment
4. Bake for 10-12 minutes, depending on how firm you like the yolks to be. If you prefer soft or runny yolks, cook 8-9 minutes.
5. Top with green onions, feta or other desired toppings and enjoy.

huevos RANCHEROS

ingredients

- chorizo sausage
- 2 eggs (or more) per person
- salsa or enchilada sauce
- guacamole
- sour cream *(optional)*
- cheese *(optional)*

directions

1. Cook the sausage in a medium pan and set aside
2. Lower heat and drop eggs into the same pan without breaking yolks. Cook until yolks are mostly set but still slightly runny.
3. Put eggs on plate, top with sausage, salsa or sauce, guacamole, and cheese and sour cream if desired.

brain power SMOOTHIE

ingredients

- 2 cups coconut milk
- 1/4 cup coconut oil
- 2 tablespoons gelatin powder
- 1/2 teaspoon vanilla
- 1 banana *(optional)*

- 2 or more egg yolks
- 1 cup ice
- flavor of choice: 1 tablespoon organic cocoa powder, 1/2 cup strawberries, 1 teaspoon cinnamon, etc.

directions

1. Put all ingredients into blender or Vitamix and blend until smooth.

2. Wasn't that easy?!

homemade SAUSAGE

ingredients

- 2 pounds of ground pork (*or two pounds of boston butt, finely ground*)

- 1 tablespoon himalayan salt or sea Salt

- 2 teaspoons ground black pepper

- 2 teaspoons finely chopped fresh sage leaves or 1 teaspoon of dried ground sage

- 1 teaspoon dried fennel, crushed

- 1 teaspoon garlic powder

- 1/2 teaspoon dried rosemary leaves

- 1 teaspoon fresh thyme or 1/2 teaspoon dried thyme leaves

- *Optional:* A dash of cayenne pepper and cloves (*about 1/8 teaspoon of each*)

directions

1. Grind meat with the finest blade of the grinder (*if grinding yourself*).

2. Combine ground pork with other ingredients and mix well.

3. Form in to 16 one-inch patties.

4. Store in the fridge or freezer until ready to use.

5. To cook: heat in skillet over medium heat for 5-7 minutes per side until cooked through.

sweet potato, sausage, and apple HASH

ingredients

- 4 sweet potatoes, peeled and chopped
- 2 granny smith apples, cored and chopped
- 2 onions, finely chopped
- 1 pound organic sausage
- 1 teaspoon each of salt, pepper and garlic powder *(or to taste) (divided)*
- 1/4 cup coconut oil, divided

directions

1. Preheat the oven to 400 degrees F.

2. Cut sweet potatoes in to large chunks and place on baking sheet. Drizzle with 2 tablespoons of coconut oil oil and sprinkle with spices to taste. Toss to coat. Roast the sweet potatoes until they are soft but not mushy, about 10 to 15 minutes. Remove from the oven and reserve.

3. While that is cooking, coat a large saute pan with coconut oil. Add the sausage and turn on medium heat. When the sausage has started to get crispy and brown, add the onions, season with salt and saute until the onions are very soft and translucent Add the apples sauté an additional 3 to 4 minutes.

4. Pour this mixture over the sweet potato mixture and add to the oven for an additional 7-10 minutes or until sweet potatoes are soft and starting to brown.

appetizers and snacks

"Why not go out on a limb?
Isn't that where the fruit is?"

- Frank Scully, author

recipes

- -

bacon chicken BITES

ingredients

- 1 pound chicken breast (*pastured*)
- 1 package of nitrate free bacon
- 3 tablespoons dijon mustard
- 3 tablespoons raw honey
- 1 teaspoon garlic powder
- 1/2 teaspoon salt
- 1/2 teaspoon pepper

directions

1. Preheat the oven to 425 degrees F.
2. Cut the bacon slices in to thirds.
3. Cut the chicken in to bite-size pieces.
4. Wrap each chicken piece with a piece of bacon and secure with a toothpick if needed.
5. Place in an oven safe dish (*preferably with a rack to keep them off the bottom, but this is not required*)
6. Mix mustard, honey, and spices and pour/rub on top of each piece of bacon/chicken.
7. Bake for 25-30 minutes or until bacon is browned and chicken is completely cooked.
8. Cool slightly and serve.
9. TIP: For extra flavor, garnish with a little goat cheese.
10. Enjoy!

crispy kale CHIPS

ingredients

- one bunch of kale
- 3 tablespoons olive oil
- sea salt
- baking sheet
- pastry brush *(or piece of cloth, or fingers)*

directions

1 Preheat to oven to 370 degrees F.

2 Make sure kale leaves are washed and dried well. Remove stems- this is optional, and we actually often leave them in and just eat the leaves off of the stems.

3 Brush or rub the leaves with olive oil until well coated and sprinkle with sea salt to taste.

4 Place in the preheated oven for 5-10 minutes or less depending on how hot your oven is. You will need to watch them closely and remove them as soon as they are crispy and barely browning.

5 Serve immediately or leave on the counter on a plate *(do not cover)* for up to 3 days.

6 Flavor variations: try adding spices like cumin and chili powder or ginger and garlic for a different taste.

ground beef JERKY

ingredients

- 2-3 pounds of grass fed ground beef *(or venison, elk, bison, etc.)*
- 1-3 tablespoons sea salt *(to taste)*
- pepper *(to taste)*
- garlic powder
- coconut aminos *(optional)*
- other spices to taste. I've made a Mexican type flavor with cumin and cilantro; a Chinese variation with ginger and fermented soy sauce; and an Italian version with oregano, basil, marjoram, extra garlic and pepper.

directions

1. Preheat the oven to its lowest setting. On my oven this is 170 degrees F.

2. Lightly rub olive oil over the bottom of a large baking sheet with a lip. *(It is ok to use olive oil here because we aren't heating to high temps!)*

3. Mix any desired spices in with the ground meat

4. Using the side of a glass or a rolling pin, roll the meat evenly around the baking sheet. It should be around 1/4 inch thick. If it is too thick, use a second baking sheet.

5. Using a butter knife, lightly score the meat to make the sizes you want for the jerky. You can also skip this step and use kitchen scissors to cut into strips when its done.

6. Brush with coconut aminos or fermented soy sauce if desired and sprinkle with a little extra sea salt. *(I use Himalayan salt which has almost 90 trace minerals)*

7. Put in the oven for 8-12 hours or until hardened. It is a good idea to flip once, but not necessary at all. I usually stick this in at night and it is ready to flip in the morning and done a few hours later.

8. Store out of the fridge for a couple weeks, or keep in the freezer if you aren't going to use it before then.

bacon wrapped SALMON CAKES

ingredients

- 2 pounds of wild caught fresh, frozen or 2 cans wild caught salmon
- 1 package of bacon
- 1/4 cup very finely diced onion
- 1/4 cup very finely diced bell pepper (optional)
- 2 minced garlic cloves
- 3 tablespoons parmesan cheese (optional)

- 1 egg
- 2 teaspoons mustard (Dijon is best)
- Spices of choice (I use salt, pepper, garlic, and herb blend)
- 1 bunch asparagus
- 2 yellow squash or zucchini
- 1 onion

directions

1 Preheat oven to 350 degrees F.

2 Cook salmon in skillet (heat canned salmon if using to cook off the juice) You want it to be flaky and have no extra juice.

3 Let salmon cool while dicing onion, garlic, bell pepper, etc.

4 Mix cooled salmon with onion, bell pepper, garlic, parmesan, egg, mustard and spices to make a thick mixture

5 Cut bacon slices in half. Lay bacon slices on buttered cookie sheet with rim. Use your hand to scoop about 1/4 cup of salmon mixture and roll into a ball. Wrap the bacon around the salmon and pin with toothpick (not necessary, but makes eating easier)

6 Place on cookie sheet and repeat until all salmon mixture is used up

7 Place into oven and cook about 15-20 minutes until cooked through and until bacon is crispy

8 While those are cooking, sauté peeled and sliced squash/zucchini and onion into skillet with butter and spices and cook until soft

9 Boil asparagus for 2-3 minutes, remove from water and sauté with butter and spices (garlic and salt) in same skillet (get squash mix out first) for 1 minute or so.

greek MEATBALLS

ingredients

- 1 pound ground turkey (or other ground meat, but turkey is best in this recipe)
- 1 large onion, grated
- 1/4 cup almond flour
- 1 tablespoon finely chopped fennel greens
- 1 tablespoon finely chopped fennel bulb
- 2 eggs
- 1 tablespoon lemon juice
- 1 teaspoon lemon zest
- pinch (1/4 teaspoon) fresh mint, very finely diced (or dried, use slightly less)
- 1 clove of minced garlic
- 1 teaspoon garlic powder
- salt and pepper to taste
- sauce: 1 cup greek yogurt, 1 tablespoon minced garlic or 1/2 teaspoon garlic powder, pinch of salt, 1 teaspoon of lemon juice, 1 cucumber (finely chopped)

directions

1. Pre-heat oven to 350 degrees F.

2. In a large bowl, mix the grated onion, ground turkey, almond flour, fennel greens, fennel bulb, egg, lemon juice and zest, mint, garlic, salt and pepper with hands. Add any extra almond flour if needed to make thick enough to form into meat balls.

3. Form into about 1 inch meatballs and place on an oiled baking sheet or in a large baking dish.

4. Place in the oven for approximately 30-40 minutes or until cooked through.

5. While baking, mix the ingredients for the sauce and prepare salad of choice.

6. Serve meatballs with the yogurt sauce and salad on the side. The yogurt dip also makes a great salad dressing.

7. Enjoy!

ingredients

- About half a pound of mozzarella cheese, cut into sticks
- 2 eggs
- 1/2 cup (*or more*) of almond flour
- 1 teaspoon of Italian seasoning
- 1/2 teaspoon Himalayan salt
- 1-2 cups of tallow, lard or coconut oil for frying (*I prefer tallow*)

directions

1 The day before you are planning to make, or at least 3-4 hours before, put cheese sticks in the freezer on a plate.

2 Once cheese is completely frozen, crack eggs into a medium bowl and beat with about a teaspoon of water until creamy.

3 Combine the almond flour, italian seasoning and salt on a medium plate.

4 Put the tallow, lard or oil in a small pan so that it is about an inch deep and bring to medium high heat.... it needs to be hot before the cheese goes in.

5 Remove the cheese from the fridge and dip the cheese in the egg mixture, then in the almond flour mixture, then back in the egg mixture and repeat if necessary until well coated. They need to be coated completely so they seal and the cheese can't escape.

6 Drop 3 or 4 at a time into the heated oil for a couple of minutes until they are starting to brown and carefully remove. I removed them with a flat pasta scoop (finally, a good use for it) but a slotted spoon will work too... you just don't want to squeeze them with tongs or poke with a fork, as the cheese will escape and make a big mess.

7 Repeat these steps with the remaining cheese until all is cooked. Oil can be re-used.

8 Serve with homemade pasta/marinara sauce or enjoy plain! :-)

ingredients

- 1 cup water *(divided)*
- 1/2 cup *(8 tablespoons)* gelatin powder
- 1/4 cup honey or maple syrup *(optional and to taste)*
- 1 cup kombucha or fruit juice
- 1 cup pureed fruit *(strawberries and other berries are our favorite - applesauce will also work)* The easiest method I've found is to defrost frozen berries and puree them with a blender or immersion blender

directions

1. Note: It is important to have all ingredients ready before beginning as you'll need to work quickly once you start.

2. Puree fruit to create a puree the consistency of applesauce or a little thinner. For us, defrosted frozen berries pureed in a blender or food processor work perfectly. Set aside one cup of pureed fruit.

3. Set aside one cup of kombucha or fruit juice. We prefer homemade kombucha flavored with strawberries for this recipe.

4. Boil 1/2 cup water.

5. Place 1/2 cup cool water in a medium sized bowl or quart size mason jar.

6. Add 1/2 cup gelatin powder and stir quickly to create a paste.

7. Quickly add the 1/2 cup boiling water and stir again briskly.

8. This should form a thick but stirable liquid.

9. Add the honey or maple syrup and stir.

10. Add the kombucha/juice and pureed fruit and stir well. You can stir with a spoon or whisk, or use an immersion blender to make it really easy.

11. Very quickly pour the mixture in to molds or a greased glass baking dish or other greased dish and allow to cool in fridge for 2-3 hours.

12. Store in fridge in an airtight container for 1-2 weeks.

13. Enjoy!

PÂTÉ

ingredients

- 1/2 pound chicken livers (*I order from a local farmer or US Wellness Meats*)
- 6 tablespoons grass fed butter (*or coconut oil, but the taste will be different*)
- 1/2 cup finely minced onion or shallots
- 1 clove of garlic, finely minced
- 1/2 teaspoon dried thyme leaf
- 1/2 teaspoon each of salt and pepper
- 1 bay leaf (*optional*)
- 3 tablespoons brandy or scotch (*or apple cider vinegar but taste will be different*)
- 2 tablespoons heavy cream (*preferably raw*)

directions

1 Note: You can soak the livers in milk or coconut milk for a few hours (*up to overnight*) and rinse before making this recipe for a more mild flavor if desired.

2 Melt 3 tablespoons of the butter in a skillet. Add finely minced onion and garlic and cook on medium until translucent- 3-4 minutes.

3 Meanwhile, trim the connective tissue off of the livers. Add livers to pan and sprinkle with salt, pepper and thyme and add the bay leaf if using, Brown livers for 6-10 minutes until cooked on the outside and barely pink on the inside.

4 Add the Brandy or Scotch and cook until it thickens, 2-3 minutes.

5 Remove from heat and let cool for about 5 minutes. Discard bay leaf. Put in food processor or blender and puree until smooth. While blending/pureeing, add the additional butter and cream (*if using*). Add more salt and pepper to taste, if desired.

6 Once mixture is completely smooth, remove from blender and put in ramekins or a glass container and cover tightly. Put in the fridge for at least 5-6 hours or overnight (*preferred*) to harden and let flavors meld. Serve with homemade grain free crackers or vegetables. I like to make vegetable chips by cooking turnips and beets in coconut oil and serve on that.

meats and mains

"Cooking is like love. It should be entered into with abandon or not at all."

- Harriet Van Horne

recipes

ingredients

- 2-3 medium sized eggplants
- salt
- about 1/2 cup coconut flour (*or almond flour*)
- 1/3 cup arrowroot powder (*can use more coconut if you don't have this*)
- garlic, salt, pepper and basil leaf

- 3-4 eggs
- 1 tablespoon heavy cream (*optional*)
- 1 jar (*24 ounces*) of pasta sauce (*check ingredients!*)
- Parmesan cheese
- Mozzarella cheese
- tallow, lard or coconut oil

directions

1. About an hour before preparing, peel eggplant and slice into 1/4 to 1/2 inch slices. Place eggplant in strainer and sprinkle heavily with salt. Let sit for 45 mins to 1 hour. This sweats the eggplant and makes it much less bitter. Rinse well with water and pat dry

2. Put lard, tallow or coconut oil (*about 1-2 cups*) in a large skillet and turn on medium heat.

3. Preheat oven to 350 degrees F.

4. Mix coconut flour, arrowroot, 2 tablespoons parmesan and spices in large bowl or on a large plate

5. Beat eggs with heavy cream, if using

6. Dip eggplant in egg mixture, then in coconut flour mixture and place in hot oil in skillet

7. Cook approximately 4 minutes per side until browned

8. As eggplant is finished, place in a 13x9 baking dish

9. Pour pasta sauce over the eggplant and then top with parmesan and mozzarella, if desired

10. Heat in oven until cheese is melted and sauce is heated.

stuffed sweet POTATOES

ingredients

- 1 pound ground sausage of choice
- 4 handfuls of raw spinach *(about one bag or bunch)*
- 2 onions
- 4-6 medium/large sweet potatoes

- salt, pepper, garlic powder, sage, and basil to taste
- Optional toppings - raw, sharp cheddar cheese, sour cream, cream cheese

directions

1. Bake sweet potatoes for 45 minutes to an hour until soft *(can be done ahead of time and re-heated)*

2. Brown sausage in a large skillet.

3. When it is almost browned, dice onion and add.

4. When onions have started to soften, add the spinach.

5. Saute until all are cooked and spice to taste.

6. When sweet potatoes are soft, remove and cut in half lengthwise.

7. In a large baking dish or on a baking sheet, Flatten the sweet potato a little bit and add a big scoop of the stuffing mixture to the middle of the sweet potato, evenly dividing among them.

8. Top with cheese *(if using)*

9. Return to the oven for about 10 minutes to incorporate flavors and melt cheese.

10. Top with sour cream *(optional)* and serve.

stuffed sausage B O A T S

ingredients

- 1 pounds ground sausage or ground beef (*preferably grass-fed*)
- 4 small to medium zucchini
- 1 onion
- 1 bell pepper
- 2 eggs
- 1/2 teaspoon each of garlic powder, onion powder, salt, pepper, basil and thyme
- Grated cheese or sour cream to top.

directions

1. Wash zucchini and put into a large pot of water (*do not peel, cut, or remove ends*). Bring to a boil and boil for about 10 minutes until somewhat tender.

2. While that is boiling, heat the oil in a large skillet and cook veggies. After veggies have cooked for 5 minutes, add meat and cook until browned.

3. Once zucchini are cooked, cut in half lengthwise and scoop out the seeds. Preheat the oven to 375 degrees F.

4. Place zucchini on large baking sheet and add the scooped out seeds to the meat and veggies mixture. Add the roasted red peppers and the egg(s) to the (*somewhat cooled*) meat mixture and stir well. Evenly divide the meat mixture and "stuff" it into the zucchini boats.

5. Top each with a slice of cheese (*optional*) Bake for 25-30 minutes or until well heated and cheese starts to bubble. Enjoy!

beef and cabbage STIR FRY

ingredients

- 1 pound ground beef (*or turkey, venison, etc*)
- 1 small head of cabbage, chopped
- 2 onions, thinly sliced
- 2 carrots, grated
- spices to taste: salt, pepper, garlic, basil, oregano, thyme, etc- I use at least a teaspoon of each

directions

1. Brown beef in a large skillet or wok, adding spices to taste as you go.

2. When beef is almost completely browned, add sliced onions and grated carrots.

3. When onions/carrots are starting to soften, add the cabbage and spice well.

4. Cook about 10 more minutes, stirring often until cabbage starts to soften.

5. Can be topped with salsa or sour cream if desired.

meatloaf CUPCAKES

ingredients

- 1.5-2 pounds of ground beef (grass-fed if possible)
- 3 eggs
- 1/4 cup almond flour (*or enough to thicken- this will depend partially on the fat content of the meat and the texture of the almond flour*)
- 1 teaspoon dried basil
- 1 teaspoon garlic powder
- 1 medium onion
- 2 tablespoons worcestershire sauce
- salt and pepper to taste
- 5-6 sweet potatoes
- 1/4 cup butter or coconut oil
- 1 teaspoon sea salt or Himalayan salt

directions

1 Preheat the oven to 375 degrees F.

2 Finely dice the onion or puree in a blender or food processor.

3 In a large bowl, combine the meat, eggs, flour, basil, garlic powder, pureed onion, Worcestershire sauce, and salt and pepper and mix by hand until incorporated.

4 Grease a muffin tin with coconut oil or butter and evenly divide the mixture into the muffin tins to make 2-3 meat "muffins" per person. If you don't have a muffin tin, you can just press the mixture into the bottom of an 8x8 or 9x13 baking dish.

5 Put into oven on middle rack, and put a baking sheet with a rim under it, in case the oil from the meat happens to spill over (*should only happen with fattier meats if at all*)

6 For sweet potatoes: if they are small enough, you can put them into the oven at the same time, if not you can peel, cube and boil them until soft.

7 When meat is almost done, make sure sweet potatoes are cooked by whichever method you prefer, and drain the water if you boiled them.

8 Mix with butter and salt or pepper if desired and mash by hand or with an immersion blender.

9 Remove meat "muffins" from the oven when they are cooked through and remove from tin. Top each with a dollop of the mashed sweet potatoes to make it look like a cupcake.

MEATZA

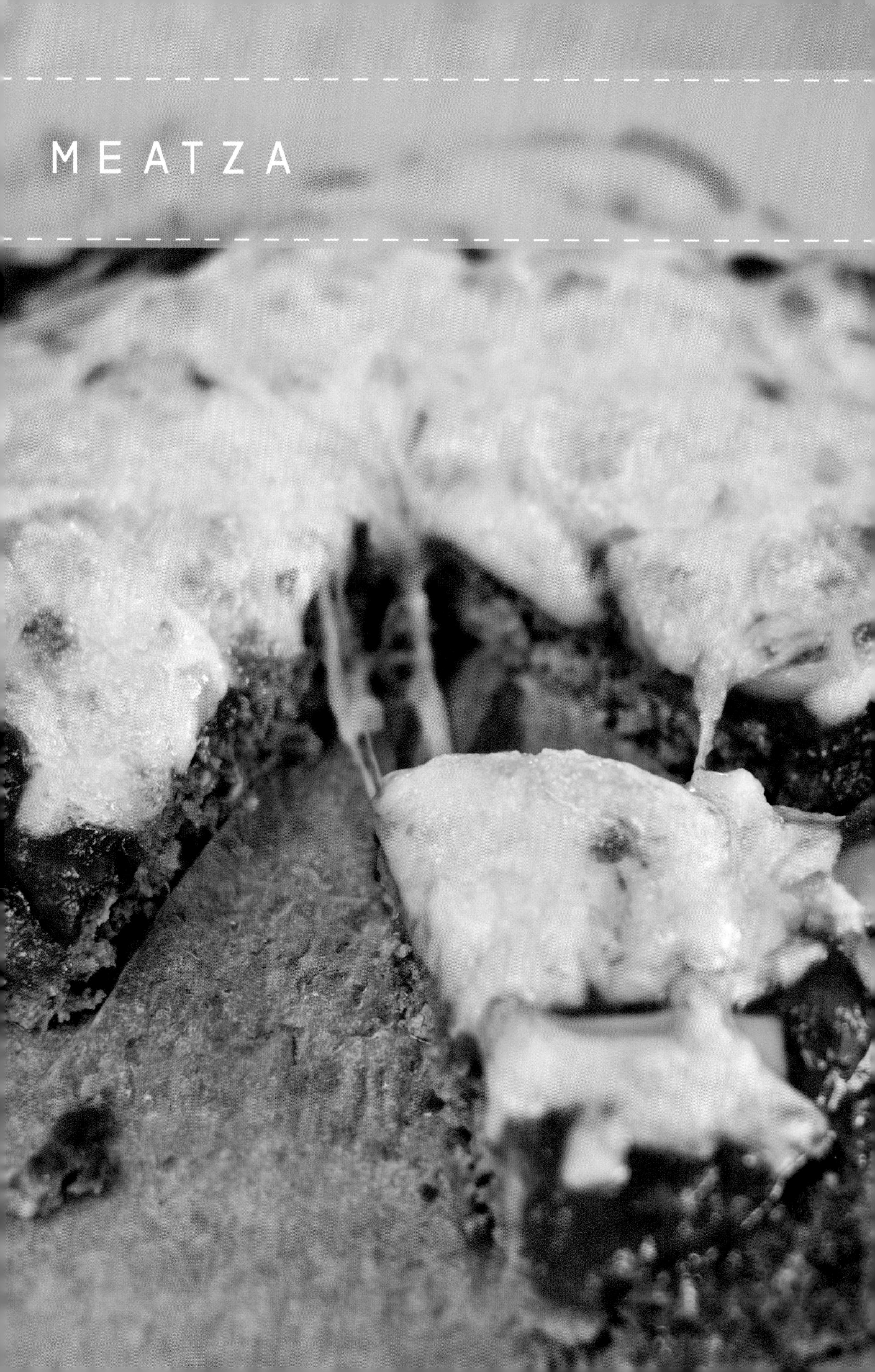

ingredients

- 2 pounds ground beef
- 2 eggs
- seasonings of choice (*I suggest basil, oregano, garlic, salt, pepper and other herbs*)
- meat topping of choice (*optional- I've used scrambled sausage, bacon, ham, leftover chicken, etc.*)

- 1/2 pound mozzarella cheese
- 1/4 cup parmesan cheese
- Jar of pasta/pizza sauce
- chopped veggies of choice (*onion, bell pepper, spinach, olives, mushrooms, etc.*)

directions

1. Preheat oven to 450 degrees F.

2. In medium bowl, mix 2 pounds ground beef with eggs and 2 tablespoons Parmesan cheese and any desired spices.

3. Mix well by hand until incorporated.

4. Spread onto greased cookie sheet (*must have a lip on the sides*).

5. Roll or press the meat onto the bottom of the cookie sheet by hand. Once oven has preheated, put meat on cookie sheet into oven and cook about ten minutes until browned and most moisture has cooked off. It will reduce in size quite a bit! Just make sure it is cooked enough, you want it pretty solid.

6. Remove from oven and put oven on broil.

7. Spread pasta/pizza sauce over "crust" then top with veggies, meat then mozzarella. I recommend putting some very thinly sliced onions on the top (*uncooked*) which brown nicely and add a nice crunch.

8. Put back into oven under broiler and watch closely. It will only need to cook 4-5 minutes. Cook until cheese is lightly brown and bubbly.

9. Remove, let cool 3 minutes, slice and serve. This is also really good cold for lunch the next day (*or breakfast!*) It has a similar texture to real pizza and tastes better, in my opinion. Serve with Salad

ingredients

- 1 pound ground beef or turkey
- 3 tablespoons ground cumin seed
- 1 tablespoon (*non-spicy*) chili powder
- 1 teaspoon garlic powder
- 1 head bibb lettuce or iceberg lettuce
- chopped tomato, salsa, onions, sour cream, cheese, hot sauce, etc to garnish

directions

1. Cook meat and season with cumin, garlic, chili powder and any desired seasonings to taste

2. Cool slightly and put into lettuce leaves like taco shells.

3. Top with desired condiments.

beef and zucchini SKILLET

ingredients

- 1 pound of ground beef
- 2 onions
- 3-4 medium zucchini
- 1/4 cup of butter
- 1-2 teaspoons minced garlic or garlic powder
- Salt, pepper, onion powder, basil, oregano and thyme to taste *(I used about 1 teaspoon of each)*
- Crushed red pepper flakes *(optional)*
- toppings: Pasta sauce, parmesan cheese, grated cheese *(all optional)*

directions

1. Heat skillet over medium high heat.
2. Thinly slice onions and add to skillet.
3. Using a peeler or food processor that can julienne, slice the zucchini into "noodles" and add to skillet.
4. Cook until starting to soften.
5. Remove from the skillet and place in a baking dish.
6. Put under the broiler and cook about 7-10 minutes until desired crispness.
7. While cooking, brown the ground beef and add spices of choice.
8. Add onions/zucchini back to the skillet, mix and serve.
9. Top with any desired toppings and enjoy!

pakistani KIMA

ingredients

- 1 large onion, finely diced
- 1 pound ground beef *(or venison, buffalo, etc) (I get from US Wellness meats)*
- 1 *(15 ounce)* can or jar of diced tomatoes *(organic, no BPA)*, drained or 2 medium fresh tomatoes
- 1/4 cup butter *(1/2 stick)*
- 1 tablespoon curry powder or more to taste
- 3-4 medium sweet potatoes, peeled and diced into small pieces
- 1 pound fresh or frozen green beans
- 1 teaspoon each of salt, pepper, cinnamon, ginger, turmeric and garlic powder *(or more to taste)*

directions

1. Melt butter in a large skillet and add diced onion. Cook three minutes or until starting to become translucent.

2. Add ground meat and cook until well browned. While cooking, add curry powder, salt, pepper, cinnamon, ginger, turmeric and garlic salt.

3. Once meat is browned, add the diced tomatoes *(drain off liquid first!)*, peeled and diced sweet potatoes, green beans and any additional spices if needed.

4. Cover pan and simmer 20+ minutes or until sweet potatoes have softened. Check after ten minutes and add a couple tablespoons of water or chicken broth if needed.

5. Serve warm and enjoy!

shepherds P I E

ingredients

- 2 (or more) pounds of ground beef, turkey or other meat

- 2-3 heads of cauliflower or 3-4 bags of frozen cauliflower

- 1 bag of frozen mixed veggies (no corn! It's not a veggie!)

- 1-2 onions

- 1 egg

- aeasonings to taste (I used natural beef bouillon, basil, garlic, salt, pepper, oregano and a little cayenne)

- 3-4 tablespoons of butter

- 4 ounces of cream cheese (optional)

- cheese to top (optional)

directions

1. Brown meat in large skillet and season to taste when cooked. Set aside.

2. Saute diced onion in skillet until somewhat soft. Set aside with meat.

3. Pour mixed veggies in the skillet to heat on low heat and in the meantime…

4. In large pot, boil several cups of water. Add cauliflower, cover, and cook until soft enough to mash.

5. Remove the pot from the heat, pour off the water, and add butter and cream cheese to the pot.

6. Add spices and mash. (I use a hand blender to make it really smooth).

7. Mixed veggies should be cooked by now.

8. Mix the meat, onions, mixed veggies, raw egg and any additional seasonings and put in bottom of 9x13 baking dish.

9. Spread mashed cauliflower mixture over it until smooth.

10. Bake at 350 for approximately 30 minutes.

11. Add cheese and bake 5 additional minutes (optional).

12. Serve warm (or reheat later).

meatloaf

ingredients

- 2 pounds of ground beef, bison, or turkey *(or a combination)*
- 1 medium onion, very finely diced or pureed in blender *(preferred method)*
- 3 tablespoons of Worcestershire sauce *(or more, to taste)*
- 1 teaspoon garlic salt
- salt, pepper and any other spices to taste- I use about 1-2 teaspoons of each
- 2 eggs, lightly beaten

directions

1. Mix all ingredients well in a medium sized bowl.

2. Place in a metal loaf pan *(if using a large crock pot)* or directly in crock pot. Place the loaf pan directly in the crock pot if using a loaf pan.

3. Put the lid on crock pot and cook on low *(6-8 hours)* or high *(4 hours)*. If not using the loaf pan, it will cook faster, so check in 3-4 hours on low or 2-3 hours on high.

4. When cooked, turn the crock pot off and let cool for 15-30 minutes with lid off before cutting.

5. Top with homemade ketchup *(optional)* and serve.

pot roast

ingredients

- 3-4 pound chuck roast
- 2 onions
- 1 tablespoon sea salt
- 1 teaspoon cracked pepper
- 1 tablespoon basil leaf
- 2 teaspoons garlic powder

directions

1. Marinate in spices at least 10 minutes, though several hours is better.

2. Brown meat on all sides in a skillet on medium-high heat to lock in juices.

3. Place roast along with sliced onions and 1-1.5 cups of water or beef broth in a crock pot or roasting pan. Cover tightly.

4. Cook for 5-7 hours in crock pot or 3-4 hours in the oven.

5. Let sit 10 minutes before cutting. Slice against the grain.

grain free SPAGHETTI

ingredients

- 1 *(or more)* pounds of ground beef *(grass fed if possible)*
- 2 medium onions
- 1 head of cabbage
- 24 ounces *(about three cups)* of spaghetti sauce *(I make my own, but there are a few good store-bought brands. Look for a glass jar with no added sugars or chemicals)*
- extra spices to taste *(basil, oregano, garlic, salt, pepper, etc)*
- 1-2 cups grated mozzarella cheese *(optional)*

directions

1. Brown the meat in a large oven safe skillet. If using grass fed, it will be lean, so add a few tablespoons of tallow or olive oil to make sure it has a little oil and doesn't stick.

2. While meat is browning, peel onions, cut in half and thinly slice. When meat is almost browned, add the onions and cook until meat is done.

3. While onions/meat are finishing, thinly slice cabbage into "noodle" thin pieces as you would for sauerkraut.

4. Add cabbage *(may have to add in several batches as it cooks down, depending on the size of your skillet)*

5. Add any spices at this point to taste.

6. When cabbage is cooked until soft and it is spiced to your taste, add the sauce and stir well.

7. If adding cheese, put on top and put into oven on broil to melt cheese.

8. Remove and serve *(with salad and a garlic version of coconut flour biscuits)*.

sweet potato LASAGNA

ingredients

- 1-1.5 pounds ground beef (can also use ground Italian sausage for part)
- 2 (24 ounce) jars of pasta sauce (check ingredients!) I used 1.5 quarts of homemade pasta sauce
- 1 large container ricotta cheese
- 1 pound mozzarella cheese, grated
- 1/2 cup parmesan
- 8 eggs
- 3-4 medium sweet potatoes (depending on size), thinly sliced lengthwise
- spices to taste (We like a lot of flavor, so I used about 1 tablespoon each of basil, oregano, thyme, marjoram, rosemary, granulated garlic, onion powder etc. and about 1/2 teaspoon each of salt, pepper, etc. Spice to your own preference!)

directions

1. Thinly slice sweet potatoes lengthwise into ¼ inch slices or smaller. Place on well-oiled baking sheet and bake at 400 degrees until just starting to brown and get tender. It isn't necessary to peel, but it might be a good idea if you are trying to hide the vegetables from any picky eaters!

2. While sweet potatoes are cooking, brown meat in a large skillet. If there is room, add the pasta sauce to skillet to warm. If not, add meat and pasta sauce to large pot and heat to a simmer. Add any desired spices.

3. Mix large (approx 32 ounce) ricotta cheese with eggs, parmesan, and half of grated mozzarella cheese. I also added garlic powder and basil to the mixture. Set aside.

4. When sweet potatoes are done, remove from oven. In large 9x13 glass baking dish (or 10x16) start layering: meat/sauce on bottom, followed by sweet potato slices, then ricotta mixture. This made 2 thick layers for me, but could be spread out into three layers if you dish is deep enough. Make sure the meat/sauce layer is on the top when done. (If you are making ahead, throw in the freezer at this point, and it will be ready to bake when you need it.)

5. When you have added all ingredients in layers, place back in oven at 350 degrees for 45 minutes to an hour or until egg/ricotta mixture is set and middle is not jiggly. It will firm up as it cools too.

6. About 15 minutes before done, add remaining mozzarella cheese to top and put back in oven.

7. Serve immediately. (I recommend a side of Italian music and a salad!)

ingredients

- 1 pound flank steak, thinly sliced
- 2 bags frozen broccoli or 1 head fresh
- 1 onion
- 3 tablespoons butter or healthy oil
- Spices to taste: I used minced garlic, 3 tablespoons fermented soy sauce or coconut aminos, 1/2 teaspoon honey and 1/4 cup beef broth with salt, pepper and ginger

directions

1 Thinly slice steak and sprinkle with salt, pepper and a little soy sauce and set aside

2 Cut broccoli into florets if using whole head and slice onion into thin slices

3 Heat oil in pan or wok

4 Mix spice, soy sauce, honey and broth in small bowl

5 Drop onions into heated pan, cook 2-3 minutes until slightly soft

6 Add broccoli and sauce/spice mix in bowl and cover for 2-3 minutes

7 Remove lid and check broccoli and onions, if broccoli is slightly cooked, add steak and cook 3-4 more minutes, stirring constantly

8 Optional: Add melted butter when it is done for extra good fat/flavor

9 Serve with salad (optional)

beef BOURGUIGNON

ingredients

- 3-4 pounds beef (roast, round, steak, etc, whatever is cheapest not ground beef)
- 3 slices of bacon
- 3 large carrots
- 1 onion
- 1/2 (6 oz) can tomato paste
- 2 cloves garlic
- small package of mushrooms, sliced
- 4 tablespoons butter
- spices (basil, thyme, salt, pepper, parsley, etc)
- 1 cup beef broth (or water)
- 3-4 cups (1 bottle) of dry red wine
- 1/4 cup almond or coconut flour (or powder almonds or coconuts in blender until finely ground)-optional

directions

1. Preheat oven to 325 degrees F.

2. Brown bacon in large pan, remove bacon and add 2 tablespoons butter to bacon fat grease in pan.

3. Cut beef into 1 inch chunks and brown beef evenly. Can roll in almond or coconut flour before browning if you are using the flour.

4. Put into large baking or casserole dish with cover

5. Chop carrot and onions and brown slightly in the same pan and then put in baking/casserole dish with beef

6. Mince garlic and sprinkle over beef

7. Sprinkle mixture with spices to taste (thyme, basil and parsley are really good additions to this)

8. Pour water or broth and wine over mixture and cover baking pan or casserole dish- can also use foil if you don't have a covered casserole dish

9. Cook in oven 2.5-3 hours until beef is fork tender and breaks apart easily.

10. About 15 minutes before beef is done, brown mushrooms in a skillet with 2 tablespoons butter. Add to beef and cook an additional 5-10 minutes in oven.

11. Remove from oven, let sit 10 minutes before serving and serve with salad of choice.

fajita SALAD

ingredients

- 2 cups of lettuce or salad greens *(per person)*
- 1/2-1 pre-cooked and marinated chicken breast (the crock pot fajita chicken recipe on page 150 is easy to make ahead)
- 1/2 avocado
- lactofermented salsa *(or regular salsa)* to taste
- Optional toppings: hot peppers, homemade sour cream, raw cheese, sweet peppers, chopped onions or other salad favorites.

directions

1. Prepare chicken ahead of time and let cool. I find it easiest to make with another meal and refrigerate so it is ready to go.

2. Place lettuce/greens on a plate and top with chicken breast, avocado, salsa and any other desired toppings.

3. Serve immediately and enjoy.

notes:

Ingredients are per person, multiply as needed for your family size.

asian SALAD

- 2 handfulls of salad greens of choice

- 1/4 cup toasted sunflower seeds or other nuts of choice *(preferably pre-soaked and toasted)*

- small handful of raisins or other dried fruit

- 4 ounces of pre-cooked meat of choice *(great use for leftover chicken or beef)*

- 1/4 cup fermented beets *(optional but delicious)*

- optional- 1/4 cup grated carrots

- Top with Asian coconut ginger vinaigrette.

directions

1. Place salad greens on a large plate and top with sunflower seeds, raisins, chopped meat, fermented beets, carrots and dressing.

2. Enjoy!

spring salad with GOAT CHEESE

ingredients

- 1 batch of homemade chicken fingers (pg. 142)
- 8 handfulls of lettuce or greens of choice
- 4-6 ounces of crumbled goat cheese
- 1 cup of toasted pecans
- 1/2 cup dried cranberries or raisins
- 1 cup sliced strawberries
- 1 batch of honey mustard dressing (pg. 142) *(or homemade dressing of choice)*

directions

1. Cook the chicken fingers according to instructions on page 142 and set aside.

2. Prepare honey mustard (pg. 142) and set aside.

3. *To serve:* Put two big handfuls of lettuce/greens on a plate. Chop chicken and top each salad with equal amounts of goat cheese, pecans, cranberries, strawberries and dressing.

4. Enjoy!

cashew chicken LETTUCE WRAPS

ingredients

- 1 pound of chicken breast or thighs, cut in to bite size pieces
- 1/4 cup butter or coconut oil
- 1 teaspoon of garlic powder or 2 cloves of minced garlic
- 1 teaspoon natural salt
- 1 teaspoon pepper
- 1 teaspoon dried basil *(optional)*

- 3 tablespoons *(or more to taste)* coconut aminos or naturally fermented soy sauce
- 3 tablespoons *(or more to taste)* maple syrup
- 1/2 cup toasted cashews
- sliced red onions for garnish
- bibb lettuce leaves for serving

directions

1. Melt the butter in a large skillet and add the chicken *(already cut in to bite sized pieces)*

2. Sprinkle with the garlic, salt, pepper, and basil *(if using)* and saute until chicken is almost completely cooked and is no longer translucent.

3. Add the coconut aminos and continue to stir until the liquid from the coconut aminos starts to evaporate off.

4. Add the maple syrup and continue to stir for another 2-3 minutes or until maple syrup and coconut aminos have cooked down and there is very little liquid left in the pan.

5. Add cashews and stir until heated.

6. Let cool slightly and serve in lettuce leaves, topped with thinly sliced red onions *(optional)*.

chicken FINGERS

ingredients

- 3 medium chicken breasts *(free range)*
- 2 eggs
- 1 cup almond flour
- 1 teaspoon garlic powder
- 1/2 teaspoon salt
- 1/2 teaspoon pepper
- 2 cups tallow or coconut oil for cooking

directions

1. Cut the chicken in to strips or nugget size.

2. Beat eggs with 1 teaspoon of water in a medium bowl.

3. Add chicken strips and toss well.

4. In another bowl, mix almond flour, garlic powder, salt and pepper.

5. Heat tallow or coconut oil in a large skillet over medium high heat.

6. Once oil is hot, coat chicken in egg mixture and then dredge in almond flour mixture and place in pan. Cook 3-4 minutes per side or until golden brown and cooked through. Remove from pan and keep in oven to keep warm while additional batches are cooking.

7. Once all are cooked through, sprinkle with additional salt and pepper and serve with *(optional)* honey mustard sauce.

honey mustard sauce:

- 1/2 cup homemade mayo (pg. 248)
- 1/4 cup mustard or dijon mustard
- 1/4 cup honey
- 1/2 teaspoon salt
- 1/2 teaspoon pepper

Mix all ingredients with a whisk or in a blender until smooth.

chicken CACCIATORE

ingredients

- 2 onions
- 16 ounce jar of BPA-free diced tomatoes
- 4 boneless chicken breasts
- 1/4 cup coconut oil
- 1 package of button mushrooms
- 1 large head of cabbage
- 1 jar of tomato paste-6 oz
- 1 teaspoon (*or more to taste*) of: basil, thyme, garlic, rosemary, oregano, salt and pepper.

directions

1. Slice onions and put in the bottom of the crock pot.
2. Chop chicken into cubes and put on top of onions.
3. Mix the tomato paste, diced tomatoes, and spices and pour over the mix.
4. Cook in crockpot on low for 6-8 hours or high 2-4 hours until chicken is done.
5. If using mushrooms, throw them in for the last 30 minutes.
6. Minutes before chicken is done, very thinly slice cabbage and saute in oil or butter until soft.
7. Serve the chicken mixture on top of the cabbage "noodles"

notes:

Can also cook chicken in the oven over onions for 1 hour if you don't want to use the crock pot.

chicken MARSALA

ingredients

- 4 chicken breasts
- 1 teaspoon garlic powder
- 1 teaspoon each salt and pepper
- 4 tablespoons butter, coconut oil, or tallow
- 1 small package of button mushrooms
- 1/4 cup marsala wine

directions

1 Melt oil/fat in a large skillet that has a lid. Cut chicken in half lengthwise to make it thinner and season with spices. Fry the chicken in the skillet for 2-3 minutes per side until starting to brown (may have to do a few at a time depending on the size of your skillet.

2 Remove chicken and add sliced mushrooms. Pour wine into skillet to de-glaze pan and stir with mushrooms for 1 minute to let alcohol cook off.

3 Return chicken to pan, cover with lid and reduce heat to a simmer. Continue cooking, covered, on low heat for 10-15 minutes until chicken is cooked.

4 Serve immediately and enjoy. I often serve with a summer salad or steamed broccoli.

spinach artichoke CHICKEN

ingredients

- 1.5-2 pounds of chicken breast, thighs or strips NO BONES!

- 1 package of frozen chopped spinach, very well drained

- 1 large *(about 15 ounce)* jar of marinated artichoke hearts *(without vegetable oil or chemical ingredients)*

- 8 ounces of cream cheese

- 1/2 cup parmesan cheese *(optional)*

- 1 cup mozzarella cheese *(optional)*

- 1 teaspoon each of garlic powder, salt, pepper

directions

1 Chop chicken into bite sized pieces, season with garlic, salt and pepper and place in crock pot for 2 hours *(on high)* or 4 hours *(on low)* [Note: This can vary by crock pot.]

2 When chicken is almost cooked, add the well drained spinach, drained jar of artichoke hearts, cream cheese, and parmesan cheese.

3 Cook for another 1/2 hour to an hour until cheeses are well melted and stir to incorporate flavors.

4 Top chicken mixture with mozzarella cheese and serve.

fajita CHICKEN

ingredients

- 3-4 chicken breasts or 5-6 thighs *(breast is better in this recipe)*
- 1 cup of salsa of choice *(look for no artificial ingredients or sugar or make your own)*
- 2 teaspoons each of: onion powder, garlic powder, salt, pepper, chili powder, cumin - or more to taste
- Optional if serving as a salad: lettuce or spinach, tomatoes, avocado, sour cream, salsa

directions

1. Put chicken in slow cooker and sprinkle with spices.

2. Pour salsa over the chicken.

3. Cook on low for 7-8 hours *(check after 5 as temp can vary a lot)* until tender. Shred with forks before serving.

4. When done, let cool slightly and serve over salad with desired toppings or use alone.

chicken PICCATA

ingredients

- 2-3 boneless, skinless chicken breasts
- 1/2 to 3/4 cup of blanched almond flour for dredging
- 1/2 teaspoon Himalayan or other real salt
- 1/2 teaspoon pepper
- 1/2 teaspoon turmeric *(optional- can add more to taste)*
- 1/2 teaspoon garlic powder *(can add more to taste)*

- 2 eggs
- 1 teaspoon water
- 1 stick of unsalted butter *(can sub 1/2 cup coconut oil though flavor will be different)*
- 1/2 cup dry white wine *(optional)*
- 1 lime
- Optional garnishes- I usually serve alone, but chopped parsley, capers and feta or parmesan cheese are good add ins!

directions

1. Preheat oven to 300 degrees F *(this is just to keep the chicken warm)*

2. Butterfly the chicken by cutting in half lengthwise and flatten using a meat hammer or the bottom of a cast iron skillet until about 1/4 to 1/2 inch thick.

3. Mix the almond flour and spices on a plate until well mixed.

4. In a bowl, beat the eggs with the water until frothy.

5. Melt 2 tablespoons of butter in a large skillet over medium high heat.

6. Dip the chicken in the egg mixture and drip well, then into the almond mixture and then back into the egg quickly.

7. Place chicken in heated skillet and cook 3-4 minutes per side until browned and no longer pink on the inside *(This may take two rounds to fit all the chicken. Use another 2 tablespoons of butter for the second round)*.

8. Remove chicken and keep warm in the oven on a baking sheet.

9. Add the wine *(if using)* to the pan to de-glaze.

10. Cut the lime in half and squeeze one half into the pan with the wine. Thinly slice the other half.

11. If using capers, drain them and add to the sauce now.

12. Reduce the mixture by about half and then add in the remaning butter until melted.

13. Remove chicken from the oven and drizzle some of the sauce over each piece.

14. Top each with fresh parsley and parmesan or feta cheese (optional)

15. Garnish with a thinly sliced piece of lime.

roasted chicken WITH VEGGIES

ingredients

- 1-2 whole chickens, organs removed
- 2-3 pounds fresh or frozen Brussels Sprouts
- 3 tablespoons Butter
- seasonings of choice (*I use salt, pepper, garlic, basil, thyme, oregano, etc.*)

directions

1. Preheat oven to 425 degrees F.

2. Wash chickens and pat dry.

3. Using hands, rub butter over the outside of the chicken(s) and place in roasting pan or 13x9 baking dish.

4. Sprinkle on any desired spices to taste.

5. Bake for 45-50 minutes, if close to being done, add the Brussels sprouts around the chicken and baste chicken and sprouts with juices and more butter if desired.

6. Bake an additional 10-20 minutes or until Brussels sprouts are tender.

7. Remove from oven, let sit 10 minutes, cut and serve.

ingredients

- 4 boneless skinless chicken breasts *(or thighs)*
- 2 apples, peeled, cored and grated
- 1 cup homemade barbecue sauce or a healthy pre-made version
- 8 slices of bacon
- 1 teaspoon garlic powder

directions

1. Wrap each piece of chicken in 2 pieces of bacon and place in the bottom of a slow cooker.

2. Mix grated apple and barbecue sauce and pour over the chicken.

3. Cook on low for 6-8 hours or until completely cooked. Can also cook on high for 2-3 hours.

4. Serve with sweet potatoes or homemade cole slaw.

chicken PARMESAN

ingredients

- 2-3 pounds of boneless, skinless, chicken breasts (or strips for the chicken fingers variation)
- 1/2 cup coconut flour (or almond flour)
- 1/3 cup arrowroot (option, can use more flour instead)
- seasonings: garlic powder, basil, salt, etc
- 3-4 eggs
- 1 tablespoon heavy cream (optional)
- 1 jar (approx 24 ounces) of pasta sauce (check ingredients if store bought)
- Parmesan cheese (optional)
- Mozzarella cheese (optional)
- Tallow, Lard or Coconut Oil for frying

directions

1. Put 1-2 cups of lard, tallow or coconut oil in a large skillet or fryer and turn on medium high heat.

2. If using chicken breasts, butterfly them and pound slightly with meat hammer or flat side of heavy spoon until about 1/2 inch thick. If using chicken strips, this is not necessary.

3. Beat eggs with heavy cream (if using) in a medium sized bowl.

4. On a large plate or dish, combine coconut flour, arrowroot, and spices and mix well.

5. Dip the chicken into the egg mixture and then into the flour/arrowroot mixture until well coated.

6. Put directly into hot oil and cook, flipping once, until both sides have browned and chicken is cooked (about 4 minutes per side on my stove).

7. While chicken is cooking, heat sauce over medium heat until warmed.

8. If making regular chicken parmesan, place chicken in large baking dish once cooked and top with pasta sauce and cheeses (if using). Heat on broil the oven until cheese is melted. For Chicken Parmesan Dippers, put the cooked chicken strips on a plate and serve with pasta sauce for dipping.

9. Serve with salad with homemade dressing of choice.

chicken broccoli CASSEROLE

ingredients

- 2 large chicken breasts (+ 2 more cooked for later in week and leftovers)

- 1 bag frozen broccoli

- 1 bag frozen cauliflower

- 4 tablespoons butter

- 1 onion, chopped

- 1/2 pound cheese (optional)

- 2/3 cup sour cream (optional)

- Parmesan topping (optional)

- Spices to taste (I use basil, garlic, salt and pepper)

directions

1 Preheat oven to 375 degrees F.

2 Bake all 4 (or more) chicken breasts in oven until cooked. Set two aside, put rest in fridge for later in the week.

3 In the same baking dish, pour frozen broccoli and cauliflower and chopped onion (butter pan if needed)

4 Put in oven until heated and mostly cooked

5 While vegetables are heating, chop chicken into bite sized pieces and grate cheese if using

6 Remove vegetables from oven, add chopped chicken, spices, sour cream, cheese and 1/4 cup water and mix well

7 Top with Parmesan if desired and put back in oven until melted

chicken SALAD

ingredients

- 4-5 chicken breasts, cooked and cubed
- 1/2 cup walnuts, chopped
- 3 large stalks of celery, chopped
- 1 medium apple, chopped *(optional)*
- 1/2 to 1 cup plain, full fat yogurt
- 2 tablespoons lemon juice
- 2 tablespoons honey *(optional)*
- garlic powder, salt, pepper, basil to taste
- lettuce or spinach

directions

1. Put chicken, walnuts, celery, and apple in bowl

2. Add yogurt, honey, lemon juice and spices

3. Mix until everything is eavenly coated

4. Serve over lettuce or spinach or wrap in leaves or romaine for chicken-salad wraps

burrito BOWL

ingredients

- 3-4 boneless skinless chicken breasts *(pre-cooked preferable)* or 1 pre-cooked whole chicken *(I make ahead on another night we are having chicken)*

- 1/2 cup salsa

- 1 teaspoon each of cumin and chili powders

- 12-15 ounces of lettuce, spinach or a mix *(enough for your family)*

- 1 tomato

- 2 avocados

- 1 cup salsa

- 1 lime

- cheese, sour cream and more salsa to top

directions

1. If cooking the chicken fresh, sprinkle with the cumin and chili powder, squeeze the juice of half of the lime over it and pour 1/2 cup salsa over it. Bake in the oven, covered for 1 hour until done, or for 3-4 hours in the crock pot on high. If re-heating pre-cooked chicken, shred with your hands or a fork and place in a skillet. Sprinkle with the cumin/chili powder, pour salsa over and squeeze half of the juice of the lime over it. Saute over medium heat until cooked.

2. While chicken is heating, make guacamole by mashing the flesh of two avocados with 1 cup of salsa and a teaspoon of lime juice. Assemble any other toppings you are serving. Serve chicken atop a bed of lettuce with any desired toppings. Enjoy! Ole!

moroccan STIR FRY

ingredients

- 3-4 boneless skinless chicken breast or thigh (*or more for leftovers*)
- 1 medium sized head of broccoli or 1 large bag frozen
- 3-4 carrots, very thinly sliced
- 1 onion, very thinly sliced
- 1 teaspoon cumin powder
- 1/2 teaspoon cinnamon powder
- 1/2-1 teaspoon turmeric
- salt and pepper to taste
- 1/4 cup of chicken broth (*or water, or coconut milk*)
- *optional toppings:* raisins and green olives
- olive oil, coconut oil or butter for sauteing.

directions

1. Chop chicken breasts/thighs into bite size pieces and saute in oil until cooked. I use coconut oil to saute.

2. Add carrots and onion and cook about 5 minutes until starting to soften.

3. Cut broccoli into florets and add to pan. Saute for another 3-4 minutes.

4. Add spices to taste and broth.

5. Cook an additional 5 minutes until all vegetables are tender.

6. Top with raisins and green olives if desired.

7. Enjoy!

sweet and sour CHICKEN

ingredients

- 1 pound of pastured chicken breasts or thighs *(boneless)*
- 2 tablespoons coconut oil or butter
- 1 teaspoon garlic powder
- 1 teaspoon sea salt or Himalayan salt
- 1 teaspoon pepper
- 1 teaspoon turmeric
- 1 teaspoon paprika
- 1 tablespoon lemon juice
- 1 tablespoon coconut aminos
- 1 tablespoon apple cider vinegar
- 1 tablespoon fish sauce
- 1 tablespoon tomato paste
- 1/4 cup orange spread *(no added ingredients - I use the Sicilian orange spread from Tropical Traditions)*
- 1/4 cup raw honey *(can sub maple syrup)*
- 1 orange or red bell pepper *(optional)*
- sesame seeds and chopped green onions for garnish
- cauliflower rice *(or white rice)* to serve with

directions

1 Cut the chicken in to bite size pieces. I use kitchen scissors for this.

2 Place in chicken in a large skillet with butter or coconut oil and cook on medium heat for 5-7 minutes or until mostly white. While cooking, add the garlic powder, salt, pepper, turmeric, and paprika.

3 After the 5-7 minutes when chicken is mostly cooked, add the lemon juice, coconut aminos, fish sauce and apple cider vinegar and cook an additional 4-5 minutes until pieces are cooked in center.

4 Drain off any extra liquid and return to heat.

5 Add tomato paste, orange spread, chopped bell pepper, and honey and cook on medium/high for another 3-5 minutes or until the sauce starts to thicken and chicken starts to brown slightly.

6 Remove from heat and serve over cauliflower rice or white rice with sesame seeds and green onions for a garnish.

greek MEATLOAF

ingredients

- 1 pound ground turkey (or other ground meat, but turkey is best in this recipe)

- 1 large onion, grated

- 1/4 cup almond flour

- 1 tablespoon finely chopped fennel greens

- 1 tablespoon finely chopped fennel bulb

- 2 eggs

- 1 tablespoon lemon juice

- 1 teaspoon lemon zest

- pinch (1/4 teaspoon) fresh mint, very finely diced (or dried, use slightly less)

- 1 clove of minced garlic

- 1 teaspoon garlic powder

- salt and pepper to taste

- Sauce: 1 cup greek yogurt, 1 tablespoon minced garlic or 1/2 teaspoon garlic powder, pinch of salt, teaspoon of lemon juice, 1 cucumber (finely chopped) (makes enough for 4 servings)

directions

1 Pre-heat oven to 350 degrees F.

2 In a large bowl, mix the grated onion, ground turkey, almond flour, fennel greens, fennel bulb, egg, lemon juice and zest, mint, garlic, salt and pepper with hands. Add any extra almond flour if needed to make thick enough to form into meat balls.

3 Form into a loaf shape and place in a loaf pan or in the middle of a baking dish with a rim around the sides.

4 Place in the oven for approximately 45-60 minutes or until cooked through. Time will vary based on how thick you make the loaf.

5 While cooking, mix the ingredients for the yogurt sauce.

6 Serve meatloaf with the yogurt sauce and salad on the side. The yogurt dip also makes a great salad dressing.

notes:

Recipe can be doubled or tripled, just adjust cooking time as needed.

smothered PORK CHOPS

ingredients

- 4 pork chops (or enough for your family)
- 2 large sweet onions, thinly sliced
- 1 cup of sliced button mushrooms (optional)
- 1/2 cup almond flour
- 4 tablespoons butter or coconut oil
- 1 egg
- 1/4 cup heavy cream (or coconut cream)
- 1/2 cup coconut milk
- spices to taste: I used salt, pepper, onion powder, garlic powder, basil, thyme, rosemary, and a tiny bit of turmeric

directions

1   Heat the oil in a large skillet over medium heat.

2   Beat the egg with about a teaspoon of water until smooth.

3   Put the almond flour on a plate and mix with about 1/2 teaspoon each of onion powder, garlic powder, salt and pepper.

4   Rinse each pork chop well.

5   Dip each into the egg mixture and then in the almond flour.

6   Put each pork chop into the pre-heated skillet with the oil and cook about 5 minutes per side (depending on thickness or pork chop) until starting to brown.

7   While the pork chops are cooking, thinly slice the onions and mushrooms if not already sliced.

8   Remove the pork chops and place on a plate.

9   Add onions to pan and sprinkle with spices.

10 Stir until caramelized and browned, about 8 minutes.

11 Add mushrooms, if using, and cook until browned.

12 At this point, scoot the onions to the side and return the pork chops to the pan. Spread the onions on top of and between the pork chops.

13 Add the heavy cream and coconut milk and any additional spices and cook over low/medium heat for an additional 5-8 minutes until most of the milk has evaporated off and started to thicken.

14 When sauce has thickened and pork chops are tender, serve each pork chop with a spoonful of the onion/mushroom sauce on top.

pork chops and APPLES

ingredients

- 4 *(or more)* pork chops *(preferably from an organic source)*
- 2 *(or more)* apples, peeled and sliced into thin slices
- 1/4 cup balsamic vinegar *(optional but good)*
- salt, pepper and rosemary to taste
- 2 tablespoons butter

directions

1 Preheat oven to 350 degrees F.

2 Melt butter in baking dish and place pork chops in.

3 Season with salt, pepper, rosemary and any other desired spices and pour balsamic vinegar over all.

4 Top with apples *(I saute them in butter first to make sure the apples get soft)*

5 Bake in oven 20-30 minutes until an internal temp of at least 140.

6 Alternatively, you could cook pork chops and apples together in large skillet. This only takes about 15 minutes.

7 Serve with salad and oven baked zucchini.

fish taco SALAD

ingredients

- 4-6 handfulls of lettuce or salad greens of choice (*about 8 ounces*)
- 1 pound fish of choice- I use cod or halibut
- 2 tablespoons coconut oil or butter - for cooking
- 2 teaspoons cumin powder
- 1 teaspoon chili powder
- salt and pepper (*about 1/2 teaspoon each*)
- 3 garlic cloves, minced
- 1 tablespoon honey or maple syrup
- 1 cup homemade sauerkraut or fermented beets
- 1/2 of a red or sweet onion, finely chopped
- 2 limes (*organic*)
- 1 orange (*organic*)
- 2 tablespoons finely chopped cilantro
- 2 plum tomatoes, diced
- sliced avocado or guacamole for garnish (*optional*)
- salsa for garnish (*optional*)
- sour cream for garnish (*optional*)
- hot sauce for garnish (*optional*)

directions

1. Melt the butter or coconut oil in a skillet.

2. Sprinkle fish with cumin, chili powder, salt, pepper, and garlic cloves, making sure that both sides are well-spiced.

3. Add fish to skillet and cook until flaky and white through the middle.

4. When fish is finished cooking, remove from heat, zest orange and lime over fish and squeeze the juice of one lime over the fish.

5. Drizzle with the honey or maple syrup and let sit.

6. *To serve:* Top a bed of lettuce with desired amount of sauerkraut/ beets, onion, cilantro, tomatoes, guacamole, and fish.

7. Squeeze juice of orange and lime over salads and top with any additional toppings.

herb roasted SALMON

- 1 filet of salmon
- 1 teaspoon each of sea salt and pepper
- 2 tablespoons olive oil or butter
- 1 fresh lemon
- 1/4 cup each of fresh, minced dill, parsley and green onions
- 1/4 cup dry white wine or cooking wine

directions

1. Preheat the oven to 425 degrees F.

2. Place the salmon fillet in a glass baking dish and sprinkle with salt and pepper. Drizzle with olive oil and squeeze fresh lemon juice over it. Let it stand at room temperature for 15 minutes.

3. Stir together the fresh minced green onions, dill, and parsley and pour around the salmon.Pour white wine on salmon.

4. Roast in preheated oven for 10 to 12 minutes, At this point, it should be almost cooked except for a small part in the center. Remove and cover for 7-10 minutes or until cooked.

pecan crusted FLOUNDER

ingredients

- 4 pieces of fish of choice *(flounder, whiting or cod recommended)*
- 1/4 cup of butter
- 2 eggs
- salt, pepper, and garlic, to taste
- 1 cup walnuts, pecans or a mixture, ground into a meal in a food processor or blender

- lettuce or spinach
- pumpkin seeds
- 1 tablespoon olive oil
- extra pecans for salad *(optional)*
- feta cheese to top salad *(optional)*
- balsamic vinegar or homemade dressing of choice *(optional)*

directions

1. Preheat oven to 400 degrees F and make sure fish is defrosted if using frozen.

2. While heating, whisk eggs until smooth in a bowl and put walnut/pecan meal mixture on a large plate.

3. Dredge each piece of fish in egg mixture and then dip in the walnut/pecan meal mix. Nut mixture will not stick as well as flour and this is ok. You should have some leftover nut meal after lightly coating the fish.

4. Carefully place each piece in a large baking dish.

5. After all fish is in dish, put any remaining nut meal mixture on top of fish and pat down.

6. Put fish into oven and bake 15-20 minutes until cooked through and starting to flake.

7. While cooking, prepare salad by washing spinach and lettuce and topping with desired toppings: pumpkin seeds, nuts, feta cheese, olive oil, and homemade dressing of choice.

8. Serve and Enjoy

homemade FISH STICKS

ingredients

- 1-2 pounds of fish of choice *(we've used cod, halibut, tilapia and other, just make sure its wild caught)*

- 2-3 eggs *(depends on how much fish you use)*

- 3/4 cup coconut flour seasoned with garlic, salt, pepper, basil and cayenne *(totally optional)*

- 2 tablespoons parmesan cheese *(optional)*

- 1/4 cup of your fat of choice *(coconut oil, olive oil, butter, etc)*

directions

1. If using frozen fish, it is much easier to cut them with a knife while still partially frozen. Cut the fish into strips or chunks. If you use fresh fish, kitchen shears work great for cutting it.

2. Beat eggs and put in a bowl.

3. Combine coconut flour, spices and Parmesan in another bowl.

4. Dip the fish in the egg and then then breading and place in skillet with the oil of your choice on medium to medium high heat. (Tip: have the pan hot enough that oil is already melted)

5. Move the fish sticks as little as possible while cooking, as coconut flour will fall off with too much movement. flip after about 3-4 minutes, or when they start to brown. Cook approximately 3-5 minutes per side.

6. Enjoy!

fish tacos IN CABBAGE LEAF

ingredients

- 2 filets wild cod, cut in strips
- 2 eggs, beaten
- 1/2 cup *(more or less)* coconut flour
- 1/2 cup *(more or less)* almond meal
- 1 teaspoon cayenne pepper
- 1/4 cup coconut oil

- 1 head cabbage
- 1/2 cup sour cream
- 1/4 cup chopped cilantro
- 1-2 cloves garlic, chopped
- 2 limes, halved
- 1 avocado, sliced
- 1 tomato, sliced

directions

1 Peel off some larger cabbage leaves to use as taco shells. Shred the rest for filling.

2 Mix the almond meal, coconut and cayenne pepper together in a shallow bowl. Heat the coconut oil in a pan on medium heat. Dredge the strips of fish in the egg, then the almond-coconut, then place gently into the hot pan. Cook on all sides until golden brown, then place on a paper-towel-covered plate.

3 Mix the sour cream/lebne with the chopped garlic, cilantro, and the juice of half a lime.

4 Assemble the tacos by putting some shredded cabbage into a cabbage leaf, add a few strips of fish, some slices of avocado, and top with the sour cream mixture and a squeeze of lime juice.

parsnip shrimp LO MEIN

ingredients

- 1 pound of fresh parsnips
- 2 cups of chopped green beans *(fresh or frozen)*
- 1 carrot, chopped *(optional)*
- 1 onion, thinly sliced
- 1 pound pre-cooked shrimp *(fresh or frozen)*
- 4 tablespoons coconut oil

- 1 teaspoon garlic powder
- 1/2 teaspoon pepper
- 1 teaspoon Himalayan Salt
- 2 tablespoons Coconut Aminos *(in place of soy sauce)*
- 2 tablespoons fish sauce or oyster sauce
- 2 tablespoons honey or maple syrup *(optional)*

directions

1 I used a spiral slicer to cut the parsnips into curly noodle shapes. If you don't have one of these, you can use a peeler, or just very thinly slice the noodles.

2 Melt the coconut oil in a large pan or Wok.

3 Add the thinly sliced/chopped carrots and sauté for 2 minutes.

4 Add thinly sliced onion and green beans and sauté for another 2 minutes.

5 Add parsnip noodles and continue sautéing on medium heat for 5-8 minutes until all ingredients are starting to soften.

6 Add the garlic powder, pepper, salt, coconut aminos, fish sauce and honey and stir well.

7 If using pre-cooked frozen shrimp, add them now and put a lid on the pan to help them heat up.

8 If using defrosted pre-cooked shrimp, wait an additional 2 minutes.

9 Continue cooking until shrimp are hot and vegetables are all tender. Serve immediately.

shrimp carbonara with
SWEET POTATO NOODLES

ingredients

- 3-4 medium sweet potatoes
- 1 pound wild-caught shrimp
- 4 tablespoons butter or coconut oil
- 6 slices of bacon
- 1 cup of peas or chopped asparagus spears

- 1/2 cup parmesan cheese *(optional)*
- 1/2 cup heavy cream or coconut milk
- 1 onion
- spices to taste: I used 1 teaspoon each of garlic powder, Italian seasoning, salt and Pepper

directions

1. Peel the sweet potatoes and using a peeler or food processor that can julienne *(if you have one)* thinly slice it into noodle-like strips. This will take a while with a peeler, but is a good job for an older child to help with. Once all the sweet potatoes are peeled, melt 3 tablespoons of the butter or coconut oil in a large skillet and add the sweet potato "noodles." Sprinkle lightly with sea salt or Himalayan Salt.

2. Cook for about 7-8 minutes, stirring constantly, until noodles are starting to get tender but are not mushy yet. Remove from pan. Add the bacon and cook until crispy. Remove from pan and add onion, peas/asparagus and the remaining tablespoon of butter or oil if needed. Cook 3-4 minutes or until onions are translucent and peas are bright green and tender. Add the shrimp *(tails and skins removed)* and saute another 5-6 minutes until shrimp is cooked *(less time if shrimp is pre-cooked)*. Add the parmesan and cream/coconut milk and desired spices to taste. Stir 1-2 minutes to thicken. *(can completely omit the parmesan and cream/coconut milk if you don't want a creamy pasta and prefer a stir-fry type taste)*

curried SHRIMP AND VEGETABLES

ingredients

- 1 pound shrimp *(frozen or fresh, tails removed)*
- 1 onion
- 3 tablespoons butter or coconut oil
- 1-3 teaspoons of curry powder *(if you don't like this, just sauté the shrimp in butter and add spices you do like)*
- 1 cup coconut milk *(can or carton)*
- 1 bag frozen cauliflower or veggies of choice

directions

1. Melt butter or oil in skillet and add sliced onion

2. Cook until slightly soft and add coconut milk, curry seasoning and other spices if desired

3. Cook a couple minutes to incorporate flavors

4. Add shrimp *(thaw if frozen)* and cook approximately 5 minutes until shrimp are cooked

5. Serve with steamed veggies of choice topped with butter and salad with homemade dressing

soups
and
stews

"You don't have to cook fancy or complicated masterpieces — just good food from fresh ingredients."

- Julia Child

recipes

ingredients

- 2 pounds *(or more)* of bones from a healthy source
- 2 chicken feet for extra gelatin *(optional)*
- 1 onion
- 2 carrots
- 2 stalks of celery
- 2 tablespoons apple cider vinegar
- *optional:* 1 bunch of parsley, 1 tablespoon or more of sea salt, 1 teaspoon peppercorns, additional herbs or spices to taste. I also add 2 cloves of garlic for the last 30 minutes of cooking.

directions

1   If you are using raw bones, especially beef bones, it improves flavor to roast them in the oven first. I place them in a roasting pan and roast for 30 minutes at 350.

2   Place the bones in a large stock pot *(I use a 5 gallon pot)*. Pour *(filtered)* water over the bones and add the vinegar. Let sit for 20-30 minutes in the cool water. The acid helps make the nutrients in the bones more available. Rough chop and add the vegetables *(except the parsley and garlic, if using)* to the pot. Add any salt, pepper, spices, or herbs, if using.

3   Bring the broth to a boil. Once it has reached a vigorous boil, reduce to a simmer and simmer until done. These are the times I simmer for: Beef broth/stock: 48 hours; Chicken or poultry broth/stock: 24 hours; Fish broth: 8 hours

4   During the first few hours of simmering, you'll need to remove the impurities that float to the surface. A frothy/foamy layer will form and it can be easily scooped off with a big spoon. Throw this part away. I typically check it every 20 minutes for the first 2 hours to remove this. Grass-fed and healthy animals will produce much less of this than conventional animals.

5   During the last 30 minutes, add the garlic and parsley, if using.

6   Remove from heat and let cool slightly. Strain using a fine metal strainer to remove all the bits of bone and vegetable. When cool enough, store in a gallon size glass jar in the fridge for up to 5 days, or freeze for later use.

sweet potato SOUP

ingredients

- 1 medium to large winter squash or pumpkin
- 3-4 medium sweet potatoes
- 1/4 cup of coconut oil or butter
- 2 onions
- 1 quart chicken broth or stock (*homemade if possible*)
- 2 cups coconut milk (*or water*)
- 1 pound of meat of choice: leftover chicken, sausage, ground beef or bacon all work
- *Optional garnishes:* crumbled bacon, cheese, chopped green onions

directions

1. Peel and chop the squash and sweet potatoes.

2. In a large pot, boil at least 2 quarts of water and add the chopped squash and sweet potatoes. Cook until fork tender and remove.

3. Let cool slightly. Using a blender, hand blender of food processor, blend half of the cooked squash/sweet potatoes with the broth, coconut milk and spices until smooth and return it to the pot.

4. Add the other half of the cooked squash/sweet potatoes.

5. In a large skillet, brown the meat you are using if not already cooked (*I like ground sausage*) and add to pot when cooked.

6. Thinly slice onions and cook in the skillet with coconut oil or butter if needed until soft. Add to pot.

7. Cook bacon in skillet if using for a garnish.

8. Heat pot on low heat until ingredients are mixed and warmed.

9. Serve with optional garnishes (*crumbled bacon, cheese, green onions, etc.*) and a side salad.

ingredients

- 2 pounds ground turkey or beef, scrambled and seasoned with cumin and other desired seasonings

- 2 cans diced tomatoes

- 1 small can tomato sauce

- 1 can tomato paste

- 2 onions, finely chopped

- 1 large red pepper, chopped (*optional*)

- cumin, chili powder, garlic and other desired seasonings

directions

1   Scramble the meat until browned, season as desired with cumin, chili powder, garlic, etc.

2   Dice onions and sauté in same pan until slightly tender

3   Do the same with pepper if using it

4   Add all to larger pot

5   Add diced tomatoes, tomato sauce and tomato paste and more seasonings to taste

6   Simmer 10-15 minutes until well warmed.

7   Serve with sour cream and cheese if desired

chicken vegetable SOUP

- Whole chicken or a few chicken legs or a few chicken breasts
- 3-4 ribs of celery
- 3-4 large carrots
- 2 medium onions
- 5-6 garlic cloves
- 1 package frozen spinach or 1 bag fresh
- 1 head broccoli or 1 bag frozen
- 1 package sliced fresh mushrooms *(optional)*
- any other vegetables you have around and want to add

- 5-6 eggs, beaten in a bowl
- turmeric
- curry
- oregano
- basil
- cayenne pepper
- parsley
- sea salt
- pepper
- garlic powder *(optional)*
- Other herbs to taste *(rosemary, thyme,etc.)*

1 Boil chicken in large pot until cooked. *(note: if using chicken breast instead of whole chicken, chicken broth can be used in place of water)*. Remove from water and chop into small pieces.

2 Add chopped celery, carrots, onions, garlic cloves to boiling water. Add turmeric, curry, oregano, basil, cayenne, parsley, sea salt, pepper and garlic or herbs to the boiling water. I add 1-2 tablespoons of each except cayenne, which I add about 1/2 teaspoon or to taste.

3 Boil until vegetables are cooked. add spinach, mushrooms and broccoli. While stirring, add beaten eggs slowly so that they distribute *(it will look similar to egg drop soup)*. Boil 2 minutes until eggs cooked, remove from heat and serve.

butternut squash S O U P

ingredients

- 1 medium butternut squash
- 1 cup coconut milk
- 1 cup *(plus more to thin)* homemade chicken broth or stock
- 1 sweet onion
- 2 tablespoons of butter or coconut oil
- salt and pepper to taste
- 1/2 teaspoon nutmeg *(or to taste)*
- 1/2 teaspoon garlic *(or to taste)*
- sprinkle of thyme *(optional)*

directions

1. Cut top and bottom off of butternut squash and use knife to carefully cut remaining skin off.

2. Cut in half and scoop out seeds *(they are great roasted!)*

3. Chop squash into small cubes and dice onion.

4. In a large stock pot, melt the butter and add diced onion.

5. Saute 3 minutes until starting to soften and add squash.

6. Saute an additional 5 minutes until squash starts to brown.

7. Add coconut milk, stock, and spices and bring to simmer.

8. Simmer about 20 minutes until soft.

9. Use a blender or hand blender to puree until smooth.

10. Serve warm or make ahead to reheat for a fast meal addition.

carrot ginger S O U P

ingredients

- 1 leek
- 1/4 cup coconut oil
- 2 pounds carrots
- 2 sweet potatoes
- 2 garlic cloves, peeled and minced
- 2 tablespoons grated fresh ginger root
- 1/2 teaspoon curry powder
- 5 cups chicken stock
- 1 teaspoon salt
- 1/2 teaspoon pepper

directions

1 Trim off the tough green end of leek, then slice leek lengthwise and rinse out. Slice leek halves into 1/4-inch slices.

2 Trim carrots, wash and slice diagonally. Peel sweet potato and cut into 1-inch cubes.

3 Pour coconut oil in the soup pot and sauté the leek until translucent but not brown. Add carrots and sweet potatoes and toss for 5 minutes on medium heat.

4 Add the garlic, ginger, and stock.

5 Bring to a boil, then lower to a simmer.

6 Cover and cook gently for 30 minutes or until the carrots are soft.

cajun GUMBOLAYA

ingredients

- 1-2 pieces of cooked chicken, chopped into pieces
- 1 pound of sliced sausage of choice *(spicy sausage works well)*
- 1 pound shrimp, peeled, talks removed *(optional)*
- 2-3 bell peppers, color of choice
- 1 onion, chopped
- 2-3 cloves of garlic
- 1 can diced tomatoes
- 2 bags frozen cauliflower *(defrosted)*
- 1 bag frozen okra *(not breaded)*
- Spices of choice *(salt, pepper, Cajun seasoning, parsley, basil, oregano, etc.)*
- hot sauce *(optional)*

directions

note:

This recipe should not be made in a cast iron skillet, as the acid in the tomatoes takes on a strange flavor from cast iron.

1 In large skillet, cook sliced sausage until browned, remove from pan.

2 Sauté chopped onions, garlic and peppers in skillet until soft, season to taste while cooking.

3 While onions, garlic and peppers are cooking, put cauliflower into food processor and pulse until it is in small pieces like rice. Can also chop with knife, though this takes longer.

4 When onion mix is done softening, add can of diced onions, okra and other spices to taste.

5 Add chicken, sausage, shrimp and cauliflower and simmer another 10-15 minutes until cauliflower is soft and shrimp is cooked. Alternatively, you can cook the cauliflower separately in some butter in another skillet and serve the gumbo over it.

6 Serve hot *(also great cold or reheated for leftovers)*

veggies and sides

"The garden suggests there might be a place where we can meet nature halfway."

- Michael Pollan

recipes

maple tarragon CARROTS

ingredients

- 6-8 carrots (*1-2 per person, depending on size*)
- 4 tablespoons of butter or coconut oil
- 1/4 cup chicken broth (*or water*)
- 1/4 cup of maple syrup (*or honey*)
- 1/2 teaspoon (*or more to taste*) fresh chopped tarragon or 1 teaspoon dried
- 1 teaspoon sea salt or himalayan salt
- 1/2 teaspoon black pepper

directions

1 Add all ingredients to a large pan.

2 Bring to a boil and cook, stirring often, for 10-15 minutes or until carrots are soft.

3 Serve and enjoy.

ingredients

- 1 bunch of asparagus (*the thinner the spears, the better*)
- 8-10 slices of prosciutto, ham or bacon
- 1/2 teaspoon of sea salt and pepper
- 3-4 tablespoons olive oil, melted butter, or coconut oil
- 1 wedge of fresh lemon (*optional*) or 1/2 teaspoon of garlic powder (optional)

directions

1. Preheat the oven to 375 degrees F.

2. Wash the asparagus and pat dry. Divide into little bunches. I usually divide one bunch of asparagus into 8 or 10 smaller ones.

3. Wrap each small bunch of asparagus in a piece of prosciutto, ham or bacon. Place on a baking sheet or in a large baking dish. Drizzle with the oil and sprinkle with salt, pepper and garlic/lemon if using.

4. Place in oven for 10-12 minutes until prosciutto/bacon/ham is starting to get crispy and asparagus is bright green. Check to make sure asparagus is tender (*not soft!*) Let sit 2 minutes to cook and serve immediately.

ingredients

- 1 head of cabbage
- 3 tablespoons *(or more)* of oil-coconut oil, tallow, etc
- Salt and Pepper to taste (I used about a tablespoon of each)
- Optional: 1 teaspoon of favorite herbs like basil, caraway seeds, dill, etc.

directions

1. Preheat the oven to 400 degrees F.

2. Slice the cabbage starting at the top of the head so that the inner pieces for circles within the slices. Aim for 1/4-1/2 inch slices.

3. Oil a baking sheet with 1 tablespoon of the oil. Place the cabbage on the baking sheet and drizzle with the remaining oil. You may need to melt it if using a solid oil like coconut oil or tallow.

4. Sprinkle with desired spices *(it is even delicious with just Himalayan salt!)* and place in the oven.

5. Roast for 35-40 minutes or until tender in the middle and sides are just starting to turn golden brown. Remove and serve.

6. I enjoy this plain or topped with an over-easy egg for breakfast.

bacon and BRUSSELS SPROUTS

ingredients

- 1 pound fresh Brussels Sprouts
- 1 medium size yellow onion
- 4 slices of thick cut pastured bacon
- 1/2 teaspoon each of salt and pepper
- optional: 2 teaspoons balsamic vinegar
- 1 teaspoon coconut or olive oil

directions

1 Preheat the oven to 400 degrees F.

2 Wash and dry the Brussels Sprouts.

3 Chop in to quarters or halves (or let kids help with this step)

4 Place on a large baking sheet.

5 Slice onion and add to baking sheet.

6 Cut bacon in to 1/2 inch pieces and add to baking sheet.

7 Sprinkle with salt and pepper and toss to mix.

8 Place in oven and bake 25-30 minutes until Brussels Sprouts are starting to brown and bacon is cooked. Toss 3-4 times throughout cooking to prevent sticking.

9 If using balsamic vinegar, toss in to pan in the last 5-10 minutes of cooking to let it caramelize.

10 Drizzle the mixture with olive or coconut oil and mix well.

green bean CASSEROLE

ingredients

onion topping
- 2-3 medium onions, very thinly sliced
- 2 eggs
- 3 tablespoons of heavy cream or coconut milk
- 2-3 tablespoons of coconut flour
- 1/2 cup coconut oil or tallow for frying *(I use tallow)*

other
- 5 cans of cut or french style green beans *(can also use fresh or 2-3 bags of frozen, or 2-3 pounds of fresh just heat first to remove extra liquid)*

healthy cream of mushroom sauce
- 1/2 cup butter
- 1/2 cup cream or coconut milk
- 1/3 of onion mix above
- 8-10 mushrooms, finely diced
- 1/2 teaspoon garlic powder
- salt and pepper to taste
- 4-5 egg yolks
- coconut milk or water to thin

directions

1   Thinly slice all the onions, separate, and put in medium bowl.

2   Add the two eggs and the heavy cream and mix well until evenly incorporated.

3   Add coconut flour and mix by hand until evenly coated *(note: may use slightly more or less depending on your brand of coconut flour.)*

4   Put tallow in large skillet and turn on medium high heat.

5   When hot, add the coated onions and evenly brown, turning occasionally.

6   When browned, remove from heat and set aside.

7   In medium sauce pan, melt butter and saute mushrooms until starting to brown, then add cream or coconut milk.

8   Whisk in egg yolks and spices and about 1/3 of the onion topping mixture and continue stirring until the yolks begin to cook and the mixture thickens.

9   Add extra milk or water if needed to thin *(only a few tablespoons might be needed)*.

10 Drain green beans and pour into a 9x13 baking dish.

11 Pour the cream mixture over and mix well until incorporated.

12 Top with onion mixture and heat at 325 in oven until topping starts to crisp *(but not burn!)* and green beans are heated.

loaded CAULIFLOWER

ingredients

- 1 large head of cauliflower or 1-2 bags frozen cauliflower *(defrosted)*
- 5 pieces of bacon *(preferably nitrite free)*
- 1/2 cup *(or more)* favorite variety of cheese *(I used cheddar)*
- sea salt
- pepper
- 1 tablespoon butter *(optional)*

directions

1. Cook the bacon in a large skillet until crispy and remove bacon, leaving bacon fat in pan

2. Add the cauliflower to the pan, reduce heat to medium-low and cook until cauliflower is tender.

3. Add butter if desired and sprinkle with salt and pepper

4. Crumble bacon on top of cauliflower, and sprinkle cheese on top of that.

5. Leave on heat an additional 1-2 minutes to melt cheese.

6. Enjoy!

sweet potato FRIES

ingredients

- 2-3 large sweet potatoes, sliced into thin strips
- 1/4 cup olive oil or melted coconut oil
- Spices of choice (*I use: garlic, sea salt, pepper, basil, oregano, and thyme*)

directions

1. Preheat oven to 400 degrees F.

2. Put olive oil and spices in small bowl and mix well.

3. Slice sweet potatoes and put on large baking sheet (*or two if you are making a lot*).

4. Pour oil over the fries and toss by hand until evenly coated- this will also coat the baking sheet.

5. Bake for 25-30 minutes or more until slightly browned and tender.

6. Serve with homemade ketchup or mayo (*It is a French thing!*).

ingredients

- -

- 1-2 head of fresh cauliflower or 1-2 bags of frozen
- 4 tablespoons butter
- 2 tablespoons cream cheese or sour cream *(optional)*
- 2 tablespoons or more parmesan *(optional)*
- salt, pepper, garlic and other spices to taste

directions

- -

1. Bring a couple quarts of water to a boil in a large pan and add cauliflower.

2. Cook until tender

3. When tender, put into large bowl and add other ingredients.

4. Use immersion blender or hand mixer to blend until smooth and creamy. This is the most important step... chunks of cauliflower are a giveaway!

5. Sprinkle with extra cheese if desired and serve warm.

cauliflower FRIED RICE

ingredients

- 1 head of FRESH cauliflower *(frozen will not work)*
- 3 eggs
- 1 large carrot
- 1/2 cup frozen peas *(optional)*
- 1 small zucchini *(optional)*
- 1 onion
- 1/4 cup coconut aminos *(similar to soy sauce)*
- 1/4 cup sesame oil or coconut oil *(I get both here)*
- 1 teaspoon garlic powder
- salt and pepper to taste

directions

1. Heat a large skillet on medium high heat and add half of the sesame or coconut oil.

2. Finely chop the carrot and onion and add to pan.

3. Saute over medium high heat until starting to soften.

4. Slice zucchini *(if using)* and add peas *(if using)*.

5. While those are cooking, grate the cauliflower using a cheese grater or food processor.

6. When vegetables are cooked, remove from heat and set aside.

7. Add the rest of the oil and the cauliflower.

8. Cook, stirring constantly, for 3-4 minutes until cauliflower is starting to soften but not mushy.

9. Make a hole in the center of the mixture to reach the bottom of the pan and crack the eggs in to the hole.

10. Sprinkle with 2 tablespoons of the coconut aminos and the garlic powder, salt and pepper.

11. Scramble the eggs in to the mixture.

12. When eggs are cooked, return vegetables to pan and stir.

13. Add the remaining coconut aminos and stir until all are heated and flavors are combined.

caprese SALAD

ingredients

- 4-5 medium size tomatoes, sliced 1/4 to 1/2 inch (*good rule of thumb is one per person*)
- One slice raw mozzarella cheese per tomato slice
- 1/4 cup shredded fresh basil leaves
- 1/4 cup olive oil
- salt, pepper and garlic salt to taste

directions

1. Slice tomatoes in1/4 or 1/2 inch slices, discarding top and bottom slice.
2. Layer tomatoes and slices of mozzarella on serving dish.
3. Sprinkle with salt, pepper, and garlic salt if desired
4. Sprinkle with shredded fresh basil.
5. Drizzle with olive oil and serve.

SAUERKRAUT

ingredients

- 25 pounds of cabbage
- 1 cup *(approximate)* Kosher or pickling salt *(not table salt!)*
- large crock or container *(around 5 gallons size, needs to be glass or enamel coated)*
- 2 large plastic zip-lock bags *(2 gallon freezer bags are best)*

directions

1 Sanitize crock and utensils in dishwasher or with boiling water

2 Remove outer leaves and cores from cabbage

3 Thinly slice cabbage-using a food processor greatly speeds this up!

4 As you slice, mix 4 tablespoons salt with every 5 pounds of cabbage and let stand in a bowl to wilt a little

5 When juice starts to form on cabbage/salt mixture, pack tightly into crock using sanitized utensils or clean hands

6 Repeat this until cabbage is within about 4-5 inches of top of container

7 Pack down until water level rises above cabbage and all cabbage is entirely submerged

8 If there is not enough liquid to cover cabbage, make a brine with 1½ tablespoons salt in 1 quart of water. add cooled brine to crock until all cabbage is completely covered

9 Once cabbage is submerged, fill a 2 gallon food-grade freezer bag with 2 quarts of water. place inside another 2 gallon bag

10 Place brine-filled bag on top of cabbage in crock, making sure that it touched all edges and prevents air from reaching cabbage.

11 Cover crock with plastic wrap and cloth or towel. tie tightly.

12 Put crock in an area that will be between 70 and 75 degrees.

13 Fermentation will begin within a day and take 3-5 weeks depending on temperature.

14 After 3 weeks, check for desired tartness. If you are going to can, make it slightly more tart than usual as it will lose some tartness.

15 Once fermented, it can be eaten right away, frozen or canned according to your canner's instructions.

notes:
Do not use aluminum utensils! These quantities make enough to fill a five-gallon crock. You can adjust the recipe down and make in gallon size jars or smaller, just use ratio of 4 tablespoons salt per 5 pounds cabbage.

cucumber SALAD

ingredients

- 2-3 cucumbers- peeled or not
- 1/2 of a red or sweet onion
- 1/2 cup apple cider vinegar or white wine vinegar
- 1/4 cup olive oil
- 2 tablespoons honey or a few drops of stevia
- 1/2 teaspoon salt
- 1/2 teaspoon pepper
- 1/2 teaspoon garlic powder
- 2 tablespoons chopped fresh dill

directions

1. Cut the cucumbers lengthwise and cut in to slices.

2. Thinly slice onion into slices.

3. Place both in a medium sized bowl.

4. In a 2 cup measure, mix the vinegar, olive oil, honey, salt, pepper, garlic and dill and whisk well.

5. Pour the mixture over the cucumbers and onions and stir until well coated.

6. Store in the fridge for at least two hours to let flavors marry.

7. Serve and enjoy. Pairs especially well with grilled meats and summer dishes.

cucumber peach salad
with BASIL VINAIGRETTE

ingredients

- 2 medium cucumbers
- 4 medium fresh peaches
- 4 leaves fresh basil
- 1/4 cup olive oil
- 1 teaspoon apple cider vinegar
- 2 tablespoons raw honey

directions

1 Cut cucumbers into bite size slices and place in bowl.

2 Remove pits and chop peaches into bite size pieces and place in bowl.

3 Finely mince the fresh basil leaves and sprinkle over the peaches and cucumbers.

4 In a blender (*or using a whisk*), miix the olive oil, apple cider vinegar and raw honey.

5 Pour dressing over salad mixture and lightly toss.

roasted BROCCOLI

ingredients

- 2 heads of broccoli
- 1/4 cup olive or coconut oil
- 1 teaspoon salt
- 1 teaspoon cracked pepper
- 1 teaspoon garlic powder

directions

1 Preheat oven to 400 degrees F.

2 Cut 2 heads of broccoli into florets.

3 Drizzle with 1/4 cup olive or coconut oil and sprinkle with
1 teaspoon each of salt, pepper and garlic.

4 Put in oven for 15-20 minutes or until slightly browned
on ends.

condiments and dressings

"As for butter versus margarine,
I trust cows more than chemists."

- Joan Gussow

recipes

creamy homeade CAESAR

zesty ITALIAN

- One egg yolk at room temperature (very important it is not cold!)
- 2 teaspoons apple cider vinegar
- 1/3 cup olive oil
- 1/2 teaspoon mustard or mustard powder
- 1 tablespoon fresh lemon juice
- 2 garlic cloves, finely crushed
- 2 teaspoons Worcestershire
- 2 Tablespoons Parmesan cheese
- Salt, pepper and spices to taste.

1. Whisk egg yolk with whisk or blender on low speed.
2. Once creamy, add vinegar and other ingredients and blend until creamy.
3. Slowly add oil, stirring constantly until incorporated.
4. If it doesn't incorporate well, your egg might still have been too cold!

great with: Dark lettuces, chicken dishes, or on asparagus.

- 3 Tablespoons white wine vinegar
- 1 small squirt of Dijon mustard
- 1/4 cup olive oil
- 1/2 teaspoon onion powder
- 1-2 cloves finely minced garlic
- 1/2 teaspoon each of thyme, basil and oregano
- Salt and pepper to taste

Pull all ingredients in small jar and shake vigorously.

great with: Put all ingredients in small jar with lid and shake until well mixed.

tangy GREEK

sweet ASIAN

- 1/2 cup olive oil
- 2 Tablespoons red wine vinegar
- small squirt dijon mustard
- 1/2 teaspoon each of oregano and marjoram
- Salt and pepper to taste
- 1 clove crushed garlic
- 1/2 teaspoon lemon juice

Put all ingredients in small jar with lid and shake until well mixed.

great with Dark lettuces, feta cheese, olives, and cucumbers. Also a good marinade for a cucumber and onion salad.

- 1/3 cup olive oil
- 3 Tablespoons apple cider vinegar
- 2 teaspoons soy sauce
- 2 teaspoons honey
- Pinch of dried ginger or 1/2 teaspoon fresh zested ginger root *(preferable)*
- Spices to taste

Put all ingredients in small jar with lid and shake vigorously. You can also mix in blender or small food processor.

great with Sesame chicken (as a marinade and dipping sauce), on a spinach salad with cashews, on cauliflower fried rice.

raspberry VINAIGRETTE

balsamic VINAIGRETTE

- 1/2 cup white wine vinegar
- 1/4 cup olive oil
- 1/4 cup fresh or frozen raspberries
- 2 teaspoons honey

Put all ingredients in blender or food processor and blend until smooth.

great with: Salad with feta and cashews, grilled chicken salad, marinade on pork.

- 1/2 cup olive oil
- 1/3 cup balsamic vinegar
- One clove of garlic, finely minced
- small squirt of dijon mustard
- 1 tablespoon honey (optional)
- salt, pepper and basil to taste

Mix all ingredients in small jar or blender.

great with: Any type of salad or as a marinade on beef, chicken or pork.

FRENCH

KETCHUP

- 1 squirt of mustard
- 1 tablespoon tomato paste *(organic)*
- 1/3 cup olive oil
- 1/4 cup white wine vinegar
- 1 tablespoon of honey *(optional)*
- 1/2 teaspoon onion powder or small chunk of fresh onion

Put all ingredients in a small blender and blend until smooth.

great with: Any type of salad *(I like it on chef salads)*, kids like to dip things in this dressing.

- 3 cans / jars of organic tomato paste
- 1/2 cup white vinegar or apple cider vinegar *(this will leave a faint apple taste)*
- 1 teaspoon garlic powder
- 1 tablespoon onion powder
- 2 tablespoons honey or cane sugar, or about 1/2 teaspoon stevia powder/tincture *(or more to taste)*
- 2 tablespoons molasses
- 1 teaspoon Himalayan or sea salt
- 1 teaspoon dried mustard powder
- A pinch of each of the following *(to taste)*: cinnamon, cloves, all-spice, cayenne
- 1 cup of water
- Optional: 1 teaspoon powdered chia seeds *(powder in food processor or blender)* for thickness

Put the ingredients in a blender or food processor and blend well. Put in fridge to let flavors meld overnight or at least two hours.

mayonnaise

- 4 egg yolks at room temperature
- 1 tablespoon lemon juice or apple cider vinegar
- 1 teaspoon regular or dijon mustard (*or 1/2 teaspoon dried mustard*)
- Salt and pepper
- 2/3 cup olive oil
- 2/3 cup coconut oil (*warm*) or other healthy oil (*macadamia works well*)

1. Put egg yolks into blender or bowl and whisk/blend until smooth

2. Add lemon juice or vinegar, mustard and spices and blend until mixed

3. SLOWLY add oil while blending or whisking at low speed, starting with olive oil. Start with a drop at a time until it starts to emulsify and then keep adding slowly until all oil is incorporated.

4. Store in fridge up to 1 week.

avocado mayonnaise

- 2 ripe avocados
- 1/2 teaspoon lemon juice or apple cider vinegar
- 1/2 teaspoon each of salt, pepper and garlic powder
- 1/3 cup olive oil (*or other liquid oil*)

1. Blend avocados, lemon juice/apple cider vinegar and spices in a food processor or blender until completely smooth.

2. While blender is still running, slowly add the oil until all is added and mixture is smooth.

3. Use as regular mayonnaise.

ingredients

- 5 pounds of fresh tomatoes, peeled and seeded *(to peel, cut a small "x" on the top and drop in to boiling water for 10 seconds and drop in to an ice bath. Skin will easily peel off)*

- 1/4 cup olive oil *(or tallow)*

- 3 medium onions, diced

- 8 cloves of fresh garlic *(or more to taste)*, finely minced

- 1/3 cup fresh basil leaves, finely chopped

- 1 sprig of fresh thyme leaves *(or 1/2 teaspoon dried)*

- 1 sprig of fresh oregano *(or 1 teaspoon dried oregano)*

- 2 bay leaves *(remove when done)*

- 2 sprigs of parsley *(or 1 teaspoon dried)*

- 1 teaspoon sea salt

- 1 carrot *(1/2 should be grated and added to sauce, the other half should be added at the end of cooking and then removed)*

- 1 tablespoon honey

directions

1. Pour the olive oil into a large stockpot over medium heat.

2. Add diced onions, garlic and grated carrots.

3. Saute for 6-8 minutes or until onions are translucent and tender.

4. Add tomatoes, chopped basil leaves, oregano, thyme bay leaves, parsley and sea salt.

5. Simmer on low heat for 2-3 hours or until cooked down and starting to darken.

6. Add carrot piece for the last 30 minutes to absorb acidity.

7. Remove sprigs of herbs and piece of carrot.

8. Optional: Use an immersion blender to puree sauce until smooth *(for a thicker sauce, skip this step.)*

9. Use fresh or store in the fridge up to 1 week, or can it according to your canner's instructions for tomato products.

- 1/2 to 3/4 cup Plain Full Fat Yogurt or Greek Yogurt
- 1 teaspoon *(or more to taste)* of dried dill weed
- sprinkle of salt and pepper to taste
- 1 small clove of garlic
- 6 tablespoons olive oil
- 2 tablespoons parmesan

directions

1. Put yogurt, garlic and spices in a blender or food processor and blend until smooth.
2. Very slowly, add the oil so that it emulsifies.
3. Use immediately, or store up to 1 week in the fridge

probiotic SALSA

ingredients

- 2.5-3 pounds of tomatoes of choice

- 1-2 onions

- 4 (or more) cloves of minced garlic

- fresh cilantro to taste (I use 1/2 cup or more)

- 1 lemon, juiced

- 1 lime, juiced

- 2 tablespoons sea salt or celtic salt

- spices to taste (I use oregano, pepper, cumin, chili, and cayenne)

- peppers (sweet or spicy.. I use cayenne and habanero but sweet peppers work great too if you don't like spicy!)

- 1/2 cup whey

directions

1 Chop tomatoes, peppers, onion and cilantro and mince garlic. If you have a food processor, your could definitely use it to speed up this step!

2 Toss all ingredients into large bowl

3 Add the juice of the lemon and lime

4 Add salt and spices to taste

5 Add whey and stir well to incorporate.

6 Pour into quart of half gallon size mason jars and cap tightly.

7 Leave on the counter for approximately 2 days.

8 Transfer to fridge or cold storage

herb infused BUTTERS

ingredients

○ 1 stick *(1/2 cup)* of softened grass fed organic butter *(raw, if possible)*

○ 4 tablespoons of finely minced fresh herbs of choice *(see flavor options below)*

directions

1 Make sure all herbs and spices are finely minced.

2 Use a fork to mash together the fresh herbs and the butter until well mixed.

3 Store in a small glass jar or wrap tightly in parchment paper or wax paper.

4 Place in fridge for at least four hours *(preferably overnight)* to allow herbs to infuse flavor in to butter.

5 Use in place of regular butter in recipes or as a garnish.

suggested flavor variations:

○ One clove of finely minced garlic, two tablespoons of finely minced basil, 1 tablespoon of finely minced chives

○ The zest of one organic lemon and one organic lime *(great on fish)*

○ 3 tablespoons finely minced toasted pecans or walnuts and 2 tablespoons of honey

○ 1 tablespoon each of finely minced fresh parsley, chives, rosemary and tarragon

○ 2 tablespoons fresh minced mint and 1 tablespoon lemon zest *(great on lamb)*

○ 3 tablespoons fresh minced dill weed and 1 tablespoon orange or lemon zest *(great on fish or vegetables)*

hollandaise SAUCE

ingredients

- 4 egg yolks
- 1 stick (*1/2 cup*) melted butter
- 2-3 teaspoons fresh squeezed lemon juice
- salt and pepper

directions

1. Melt butter and make sure it is warm but not too hot.

2. In a medium bowl, whisk egg yolks with lemon juice and spices until smooth.

3. Put the bowl with the egg yolks on top of a small pan of boiling water (*make sure the bowl doesn't touch the water*) or in a double boiler.

4. Whisk the egg yolks constantly while slowly adding the melted butter in.

5. Once well incorporated, continue to whisk for 2-3 minutes (*approx*) until it starts to thicken.

6. Use immediately, or remove from heat and cover until serving.

7. If it thickens or starts to separate, mix in a 1/2 teaspoon or so of warm water before serving.

spice blends

"Once you get a spice in your home, you have it forever. Women never throw out spices. The Egyptians were buried with their spices. I know which one I'm taking with me when I go."

- Erma Bombeck

recipes

taco seasoning

- 1/4 cup chili powder
- 1/4 cup cumin powder
- 1 tablespoon garlic powder
- 1 tablespoon onion powder
- 1 teaspoon oregano leaf
  (or oregano leaf powder)
- 1 teaspoon Paprika
- 1/4 cup Himalayan salt or sea salt (optional)
- 1 teaspoon ground pepper

Put all in jar and shake well or mix in a food processor until mixed. Store in an airtight jar for up to six months. Makes approximately 1 cup. To use: sprinkle on ground beef or chicken as you would any store bought taco seasoning. 3 tablespoons is the same as 1 packet of store bought taco seasoning. Great for lettuce tacos.

curry powder

- 1/2 cup paprika
- 1/4 cup cumin
- 1 tablespoon fennel powder
- 2 tablespoons fenugreek powder (optional)- gives sweetness
- 2 tablespoons ground mustard powder
- 1 tablespoon ground red pepper flakes (optional)- adds spiciness
- 3 tablespoons ground coriander (optional)
- 1/4 cup ground turmeric root
- 1 tablespoon ground cardamon (optional)
- 1 teaspoon cinnamon powder
- 1/2 teaspoon cloves powder (optional) – adds complex flavor

Put all in jar and shake well or mix in a food processor until mixed. Store in an airtight jar for up to six months. Makes approximately 1 cup. To use: sprinkle on ground beef or chicken as you would any store bought taco seasoning. 3 tablespoons is the same as 1 packet of store bought taco seasoning. Great for lettuce tacos.

Italian seasoning

- 1/2 cup basil leaf
- 1/2 cup marjoram leaf
- 1/2 cup oregano leaf
- 1/4 cup cut and sifted rosemary leaf

- 1/4 cup thyme leaf
- 2 tablespoons garlic powder *(optional, especially if you cook with fresh garlic)*

Place all herbs in a jar and shake well. Great in any Italian recipes such as eggplant parmesan, chicken parmesan, meatza, grain free spaghetti, zucchini lasagna, etc.

rajin' cajun

- 1/2 cup paprika
- 1/3 cup Himalayan salt or sea salt
- 1/4 cup garlic powder
- 2 tablespoons black pepper
- 2 tablespoons onion powder

- 1 tablespoon cayenne pepper *(optional- won't be spicy without this)*
- 2 tablespoons oregano leaf
- 1 tablespoon thyme leaf

Mix all ingredients in jar or food processor and store in an airtight container. Good on stir frys, eggs, casseroles, and poultry. Can add more or less Cayenne to get to your taste.

ranch dressing

- 1/4 cup dried parsley leaf
- 1 tablespoon dill leaf
- 1 tablespoon garlic powder
- 1 tablespoon onion powder

- 1/2 teaspoon basil leaf *(optional)*
- 1/2 teaspoon ground black pepper

Mix all ingredients together in jar or food processor. To make into ranch dressing, mix 1 Tablespoon of this mix with 1/3 cup homemade mayonaise or greek yogurt and 1/4 cup coconut milk.

lemon pepper seasoning

- The zest from 4-6 organic lemons *(or 1/2 cup pre-dried lemon zest)*
- 6 tablespoons ground black pepper *(or whole peppercorns if you are using fresh lemon)*
- 5 tablespoons Himalayan salt or sea salt

If using fresh lemon Zest, thoroughly zest the lemons and spread the fresh lemon out on a baking sheet. Put into the oven on the lowest setting and leave until completely dried. Mine took about 70 minutes, but yours make take more or less time. When completely dried, mix with the peppercorns and salt in a food processor until well mixed. If making with pre-dried lemon peel, just mix all ingredients in a food processor until blended.

seasoned salt

- 1/4 cup onion powder
- 1/4 cup garlic powder
- 1/4 cup black pepper *(ground)*
- 2 tablespoons chili powder
- 3 tablespoons paprika
- 2 tablespoons dried parsley leaf *(optional)*
- 1 tablespoon ground red pepper flakes *(optional)*

Mix well by shaking in a jar or in a food processor. Store in airtight container.

fajita seasoning

- 1/4 cup chili powder
- 2 tablespoons sea salt
- 2 tablespoons paprika
- 1 tablespoon onion powder
- 1 tablespoon garlic powder
- 1 teaspoon cayenne powder (optional)
- 1 tablespoon cumin powder

Mix well in bowl or jar and store in airtight container until use. Use about 1 teaspoon per chicken breast or steak when making fajitas. I use for making Fajitas and Fajita Salads.

French onion soup mix

- 1/2 cup onion flakes or dehydrated onion slices
- 2 tablespoons onion powder
- 1 tablespoon garlic powder
- 1 teaspoon celery salt
- 1/2 teaspoon ground pepper
- 1 tablespoon Himalayan or sea salt (*optional but helps absorption of soup*)

Use approximately 1/4 cup per 2 cups of beef stock to make french onion soup (*add 3-4 onions that have been very thinly sliced and slowly caramelized.*) To use as a mix, you can add 1/2 cup soy-free and MSG free beef bouillon powder and use as you would a packet of french onion soup pix (*1/4 cup=1 package*). Excellent on roasts or for making french onion soup. I also use as the seasoning for the meat in shepard/cottage pie.

chili seasoning mix

- 1/2 cup chili powder
- 1/4 cup garlic powder
- 3 tablespoons onion powder
- 1/4 cup oregano
- 2 tablespoons paprika
- 1/4 cup cumin
- 1 tablespoon thyme

Mix all ingredients and store in an airtight container.
1/4 cup of mix=1 package of store bought chili seasoning.
Great for all types of chili.

Herbs de Provence

- 1/2 cup thyme leaf
- 1/4 cup marjoram leaf
- 2 tablespoons of cut and sifted rosemary leaf
- 2 tablespoons savory
- 1 teaspoon of lavender flowers (*lightly ground-optional*)
- 2 teaspoons dried orange zest (*optional*)
- 1 teaspoon groundfennel

If you are zesting the orange yourself, remove the zest of one organic orange and dry in an oven on lowest setting or a dehydrator until completely dry. Place in a food processor with the lavender flowers and lightly pulse. Remove and mix all ingredients in a jar or bowl until mixed (*do not grind up the herbs!*) Excellent in soups, on chicken or on roasted vegetables.

Caribbean jerk seasoning

- 1/4 cup onion powder
- 2 tablespoons sea salt
- 2 tablespoons thyme
- 2 teaspoons ground allspice
- 1 tablespoon cinnamon
- 1 teaspoon cayenne powder (*optional*)

Mix all ingredients together and store in airtight container.
When using, it is especially good if mixed with honey and painted on the meat.

Asian 5-spice seasoning

- 2 tablespoons anise powder
- 1 tablespoon ground pepper
- 1 tablespoon ground fennel
- 1 tablespoon cinnamon
- 1 tablespoon ground cloves
- 1 tablespoon Himalayan or sea salt

Mix all ingredients and store in airtight container. Great for recipes like beef and broccoli stir fry and other Asian themed cuisine.

pumpkin pie spice

- 1/4 cup cinnamon
- 1 teaspoon ground ginger
- 2 teaspoons nutmeg
- 2 teaspoons allspice powder
- 1/2 teaspoon cloves powder (optional)

Mix all ingredients and store in airtight container. Use as you would regular pumpkin pie spice. Great in pumpkin cheesecake, pumpkin pie, spiced pumpkin lattes or coconut flour pumpkin muffins.

desserts and baked goods

"I just figured if I was going to make the world a better place, I'd do it with cookies."

- Ana Pascal, *Stranger than Fiction*

recipes

- 1 cup of cocoa butter

- 1 cup of organic dutch process cocoa powder

- 1/2 cup raw honey or to taste- using half this amount or less will make a bittersweet chocolate

- 1 teaspoon of real vanilla extract or other flavors to taste

- *Optional:* toasted chopped almonds, orange or mint extract, etc.)

1. Melt cocoa butter in a double boiler or a glass bowl on top of a small pan with an inch of water *(make sure water isn't touching bowl)* over medium heat.

2. When cocoa butter is completely melted, remove from heat and add cocoa powder, honey, vanilla and other flavor extracts. If using a solid raw honey like Tropical Traditions, melt with the cocoa butter.

3. Make sure all ingredients are well incorporated and smooth. At this point, make sure that no water or liquid gets in to the chocolate as it can cause the texture to get mealy! Be careful even with wet hands or a drop of water in the mold! *(Note: I've also just melted all of this on very low heat in a small pan and not had a problem with it, but this isn't as reliable as the double boiler method)*

4. Pour the chocolate in to molds or onto a baking sheet lined with parchment paper or a glass pan to harden.

5. Let harden for several hours at room temperature until hardened and remove from molds. You can also stick in the fridge to harden more quickly. Will store for over a week at room temperature or can be kept refrigerated for longer.

Notes:

You can also use coconut oil in place of the cocoa butter which will produce a very healthy chocolate, but it will not be as thick or creamy *(but still very good!)* If you use coconut oil, I recommend hardening in the fridge and storing in the fridge. This is one easy way to add coconut oil and magnesium to your daily diet!

probiotic MARSHMALLOWS

- 4 tablespoons of grass fed gelatin powder
- 1 cup of water
- 1 tablespoon of Marshmallow Root *(optional)*
- 1 cup of honey
- 1 teaspoon vanilla or other flavor optionals *(mint extract, lemon, cocoa powder, etc)*

- Optional: 4 capsules of probiotics. Shelf stable recommended
- Equipment: A small sauce pan, plus a hand mixer & a metal bowl- or a kitchen aid mixer if you have one

directions

1. Optional Step: Combine 1 cup of warm water with the 1 tablespoon of Marshmallow Root and let sit for 5 minutes *(or as long as overnight in the fridge)*, Stir well and strain. Make sure that the liquid makes a whole cup.
2. Pour 1/2 cup of water *(marshmallow mix if you used it)* into the metal bowl or mixer bowl and add the gelatin. Whisk slightly to incorporate and let sit.
3. Pour the other 1/2 cup of water and the 1 cup of honey into the small saucepan.
4. Slowly bring the water and honey mixture to a boil. If you have a kitchen thermometer, you want it to reach at least 240 degrees. If not, just keep boiling, stirring constantly for 8 minutes.
5. Slowly start pouring the honey/water mixture into the bowl with the gelatin mix *(which will be hardened by now)*.
6. Turn on the mixer or hand mixer and keep on medium as the honey mixture is added.
7. When add honey mix is added, turn the mixer to high and blend with the mixer for another 10-15 minutes or until it forms a stiff cream the consistency of marshmallow cream *(it should form gentle peaks)*.
8. Add the probiotics and any flavor ingredients for the last 2 minutes of mixing *(except cocoa powder which can be added to the honey mix in the saucepan)*.
9. Grease a 9x13 inch baking dish with coconut oil, or line with parchment paper, leaving some on the sides to be able to pull up.
10. When marshmallows are whipped, pour into the lined/greased dish and smooth evenly.
11. Let sit at least 4 hours *(overnight is better)*.
12. Flip on to a cutting board and cut with a well oiled pizza cutter or knife.
13. Store in an airtight container.

notes

Do NOT store in the fridge as they will melt. Store in an airtight container at room temperature. The probiotics will decrease the shelf life to 3-4 days. Without the probiotics, these will last 2-3 weeks on the counter.

coconut CREAM

- 2 cups shredded coconut

- 3-4 Tablespoons of slightly melted coconut oil *(or more if needed)*

- 2-3 Tablespoons Cocoa Powder *(optional)* or 1 teaspoon vanilla *(optional)*- or both

- 2 tablespoons honey *(optional- or more/less to taste)*

directions

1 Pulse the shredded coconut in a food processor or high powered blender. I use a Vitamix and it works perfectly. It will be powdered at first but will start to get thicker and stick together.

2 Slowly add the coconut oil and it will form a thick, but moveable texture. If desired, add the cocoa powder/honey or vanilla/honey.

3 Blend to incorporate and store in a glass mason jar or other container.

4 Enjoy!

chocolate chip COOKIES

- 2 cups blanched almond flour
- 1/2 cup softened (*not melted*) butter or coconut oil
- 1/4 to 1/3 cup pure cane sugar
- 1 large egg
- 1/2 teaspoon baking soda
- pinch of salt
- 1 tablespoon pure vanilla extract
- 1 cup (*or less*) organic dark chocolate chips

directions

1. Preheat the oven to 350 degrees F.

2. Mix the almond flour, baking soda, sugar and salt in a bowl. Add the softened butter or coconut oil (*or a mix of both*) and stir well by hand until mixed. It should form a thick dough that is hard to stir.

3. Add the egg and mix well. This should make the dough more formable and easier to mix. If needed, add a teaspoon or two of milk or water to thin. Finished dough should be easy to form.

4. Add chocolate chips and stir by hand until incorporated.

5. Form dough into tablespoon size balls and bake for 10 minutes or until tops are starting to be golden brown. The centers will be somewhat soft, but they will continue to harden once they are removed.

6. Let cool at least 5 minutes and serve.

tip:

You can make a double batch and freeze the dough for later use.

pecan P I E

CRUST:
- 2 cups almond flour
- 1 teaspoon Gelatin Powder
- 1 tablespoons Coconut Flour (*optional*)
- ½ cup butter or coconut oil (*cold/solid at room temp*)
- 2 teaspoons coconut sugar
- 1 egg

FILLING:
- 1 cup maple syrup (*or 1/2 cup each maple syrup and honey*)
- 3 eggs
- 3 tablespoons of butter or coconut oil
- 1 teaspoon vanilla
- ½ cup coconut sugar
- 1.5 cups of pecans

directions

1. Preheat oven to 375 degrees F.

2. In a food processor, pulse the almond flour, gelatin and coconut flour until evenly mixed.

3. Add the butter or coconut oil (must be cold), the coconut sugar and the egg yolk and pulse until it forms a ball.

4. Press in to the bottom of a pie pan (*or 8x8 dish*) and set aside.

5. In a small saucepan, bring the maple syrup to a simmer and simmer for about 5 minutes or until it reaches 225 degrees (*or starts to bubble up*).

6. Pour in to a bowl and add the butter/coconut oil, vanilla and coconut sugar.

7. Use an immersion blender to combine.

8. Add eggs and blend until smooth.

9. Pour over pie crust and top with pecans (*or just dump in evenly if you don't care about the top having all the pecans facing the same way*).

10. Bake for 30 minutes or until the center is mostly set. Do not overbake!

butter pecan ICE CREAM

- 1 can of BPA free coconut milk *(or two cups fresh raw milk or coconut milk)*

- 1 stick (1/2 cup) grassfed butter

- 2-3 tablespoons real vanilla extract

- 1/2 teaspoon Himalayan salt or real salt

- 4 raw egg yolks from trusted source pastured hens (optional but really improves texture)

- 1/4 cup each of maple syrup and honey (or either one, to taste)

- 1/2 to 1 cup chopped pecans

1. Place all ingredients except pecans in a blender and blend until completely smooth. Best if butter is softened but not melted.

2. Pour in to ice cream maker or small tin can for that method.

3. Turn on ice cream maker and follow user instructions or roll/ shake the can for 20+ minutes until done.

4. Enjoy!

coconut BUTTER CUPS

- 1 pound quality dark chocolate without soy

- 1 cup of shredded coconut

- 1 tablespoon vanilla extract

- 3 tablespoons coconut oil

- 10+ drops of stevia extract or to taste

directions

1. In a blender or food processor, combine the shredded coconut, vanilla, 2 tablespoons of the coconut oil and the stevia extract and blend/pulse until thick and paste like. It will eventually start to resemble the thickness of almond butter or coconut cream concentrate.

2. Set the coconut mixture aside. In a double boiler or bowl on top of a small pot of boiling water, melt the chocolate with the remaining 1 tablespoon of coconut oil. When melted, remove from heat. Pour about a tablespoon of the melted chocolate into the bottom of 12 muffin cups (silicon work best) and rotate the muffin cup to coat the sides (I haven't tried paper liners, but they might stick!). Make sure you only use about half of the chocolate mixture.

3. Put the cups in the freezer to harden quickly once you have coated the bottom and sides of the muffin cups. When hardened, take each out and scoop out about a tablespoon of the coconut mixture into each cup and press down gently with the back of the spoon to flatten. Cover the tops of the coconut mixture with more chocolate and put back into the freezer or fridge to harden.

4. Once completely set, remove from the muffin cups (will probably need to dip the tray into hot water if using metal muffin cups) and store in an airtight container.

CRUST:
- 1 cup of almonds or pecans, finely ground in blender until flour like *(or almond flour)*
- 3 tablespoons of coconut oil plus some to grease pie pan
- 1 egg
- cinnamon powder *(1/4-1/2 teaspoon or to taste)*

FILLING:
- 1 *(15 ounce)* can of pumpkin *(nothing added)* or approx 2 cups of homemade pureed pumpkin with excess liquid drained
- 3 eggs
- 1/4 cup of honey *(or to taste)* - can substitute stevia, but the honey actually helps it hold better
- 1 tablespoon of pumpkin pie spices or about 2 teaspoons cinnamon and 1/4 teaspoon each of cloves, ginger and nutmeg
- 1 teaspoon natural vanilla
- coconut milk to thin *(no more than about 1/3 cup)*

1. Preheat oven to 325 degrees F.

2. Grease pie pan with coconut oil and mix crust ingredients by hand in a medium sized bowl.

3. Press crust into bottom and sides of pie pan and put in the oven while making the filling.

4. In the same bowl *(no need for extra dishes!)* combine the filling ingredients *(except coconut milk)* and mix using an immersion blender. If you don't have one of these, use a regular blender or food processor. A hand-mixer will not get it as smooth! It should be smooth and spreadable, but not really pourable. Add coconut milk if needed to thin slightly.

5. After 10-15 minutes, remove the crust as it barely starts to brown.

6. Pour/smooth the filling over the crust and return to oven for about an hour or until center is no longer jiggly. Will set more as it cooks.

7. Top with coconut cream or whipped heavy cream and some chopped pecans.

TRUFFLES

- 1/4 cup coconut oil *(can also use butter)*
- 1/4 cup heavy whipping cream *(organic, not whipped yet)*
- 1 1/4 cups 70% or higher dark chocolate chips
- essential oils or orange, mint or lavender *(food grade)* *(optional)*
- nuts, toasted coconut, and cocoa powder *(optional)*

directions

1. Melt the coconut oil *(or butter)* and heavy cream in a pan and bring to a strong simmer

2. Pour the chocolate in a medium sized bowl and pour the hot oil/cream mixture over the chocolate

3. Stir slowly with a whisk to incorporate until chocolate is completely melted.

4. Add 2-3 drops of mint, lavender, or orange essential oil if you want to *(mint is reaaaaaallly good)*

5. Put bowl in fridge for a couple of hours

6. When the chocolate mixture has gotten firm, remove the bowl from the fridge and using a spoon or melon spoon, scoop out small amounts of the chocolate mixture.

7. Roll into 1 inch balls using your hands and then roll in cocoa powder.

8. Can also drizzle with more melted chocolate and coat with toasted coconut, finely ground nuts, orange zest, etc.

9. Enjoy... a lot!

chocolate covered BACON

ingredients

- 1 package of *(nitrate free)* bacon
- about 1/2 cup of dark chocolate or baking chocolate *(we used 80%)*
- 1 tablespoons coconut oil or bacon grease

directions

1. Cook the bacon on a baking sheet in a 400 degree oven until barely crispy.

2. Remove and cool.

3. While cooling, melt chocolate in double boiler *(or microwave)*. If melting on the stove, add coconut oil or bacon grease to keep it from thickening too much.

4. Cut bacon into bite size strips and dump into chocolate.

5. Stir around until well coated.

6. Remove pieces and place on wax paper or clean plate.

7. Put in fridge *(or freezer if impatient)* until the chocolate hardens.

8. Confuse your taste buds!

10 minute PEACH COBBLER

- 4-6 fresh, ripe peaches

- 1 tablespoon butter or coconut oil (*per peach*) or 1/4 cup for 4-6 peaches

- 1-2 tablespoons almond flour (*per peach*) or about 1/4 cup for 4-6 peaches

- dash of vanilla extract

- If making the cream: 1 cup heavy whipping cream, 1/2 teaspoon vanilla, 4 drops (*or more to taste*) of stevia tincture. Put in blender or immersion blender and blend until creamy. Don't over-blend or you'll get butter!

1. If the peaches aren't organic or if you don't like the skin, peel the peaches and cut into slices (*about 8 slices per peach*).

2. Melt the butter or coconut oil in a skillet.

3. Add the peach slices and cook approximately 5 minutes or until just starting to soften.

4. Add the almond flour and vanilla and stir to coat peaches.

5. Cook an additional 1-2 minutes and serve.

6. Top with cream if desired.

7. Enjoy!

coconut MACAROONS

ingredients

- 4 egg whites
- 1/3 cup maple syrup or honey
- dash of salt
- 2 teaspoons vanilla extract
- 2 cups coconut flakes
- 1 tablespoon coconut oil or butter
- Optional: 1 tablespoon of Maca Powder

directions

1. Whisk the egg whites with a dash (1/4 teaspoon) salt until stiff.

2. Add honey, vanilla, coconut, melted coconut oil and Maca *(if using)*.

3. Carefully fold into egg whites.

4. Let the mixture rest in the fridge for 30 minutes so that the coconut can soak up the mixture.

5. Preheat the oven to 350 degrees F.

6. Gently spoon in 1 tablespoon scoops on to parchment paper lined baking sheet.

7. Bake for 8-12 minutes until just starting to brown.

drinks

"You can never get a cup of tea large enough
or a book long enough to suit me."

- C.S. Lewis

recipes

ingredients

- gallon size glass jar *(make sure its really clean!!)*

- 1 gallon of brewed sweetened tea *(ratio: 1 cup of sugar per gallon of tea)* I use regular black tea, though I've heard of others using green or herbal teas

- a SCOBY and 1/2 cup of liquid from a previous batch of Kombucha

- coffee filter or thin cloth and a rubber band

directions

1 Prepare the sweet tea. I use 1 family size tea bag or 8-10 small bags per gallon of water. Add 1 cup of regular sugar *(organic preferably)*. Do not use honey!

2 Let tea cool to room temperature and make sure it is really cool! This step is very important as too hot of tea can kill your SCOBY.

3 Once tea is completely cool, pour into glass jar, leaving just over an inch of room at the top. Pour in 1/2 cup liquid from a previous batch of Kombucha or if starting from a dehydrated SCOBY, pour in 1/2 cup from a store-bought bottle of Kombucha.

4 With very clean hands, gently place the SCOBY at the top of the jar of tea. It should float, though if it doesn't just let it fall and don't stick your hands in the tea!

5 Cover the jar with the coffee filter or cloth and rubber band tightly *(flies love this stuff!)*

6 Put the jar in a warm *(around 70-75 degrees is best)* corner of the kitchen where it is at least a few feet away from any other fermenting products.

7 Let sit to ferment for around 7 days, though the length of time may vary depending on your temperature. You can test the Kombucha by placing a straw in the jar carefully *(slide under the SCOBY)* and sipping. It should taste tart but still very slightly sweet also.

8 At this point, Kombucha is ready for a second ferment. If you aren't doing the second ferment, just pour the kombucha into another jar or jars with airtight lids and seal until ready to drink.

probiotic beet K V A S S

ingredients

- 2-4 beets
- 1/4 cup whey or juice from sauerkraut
- 1 tablespoon sea salt or himalayan salt
- filtered water
- half gallon glass jar

directions

1. Wash beets and peel *(if not organic)* or leave skin on *(if organic)*

2. Chop beet in to small cubes but don't grate.

3. Place beets in bottom of half gallon jar.

4. Add whey/sauerkraut juice and salt *(If you don't want to use whey or sauerkraut juice, you can double the salt instead, though it may take longer to ferment)*

5. Fill jar with filtered water.

6. Cover with a towel or cheesecloth and leave on the counter at room temperature for 2 days to ferment.

7. Transfer to fridge.

8. Consume as desired. I drink 3-4 ounces each morning and night.

dairy free WATER KEFIR

- Hydrated water kefir grains (at least two teaspoons)

- 1/4 cup sugar per quart of water (*I like organic unprocessed Rapadura sugar*) Do not use honey!!

- Non-chlorinated filtered water (*If you use reverse osmosis, consider adding a few drops of trace minerals back in or sticking a rinsed pastured egg shell in for minerals*) If you just have tap water, boil it to remove chlorine and cool before using

directions

Dissolve the sugar in small amount of hot water. When sugar is dissolved, fill the rest of the jar with cool filtered water and make sure the water is not warm- it must be at room temp! Add the hydrated water kefir grains Cover with towel, cheesecloth, or coffee filter and rubber band to keep out insects or small children. Leave on the counter (*preferably at 70-75 degrees*) for 24-48 hours. The longer you leave it, the more sugar ferments out, so if you ware limiting carbs, I recommend 48 hours. Don't leave longer than this! It can starve the grains! After 48 hours, strain the water kefir grains through a bamboo or mesh strainer (*don't use metal if you can help it!*) pouring the liquid into another container. I use a half gallon jar for the first process and strain into two quart size jars. Restart the process by dissolving more sugar in water, adding cool water and adding Water Kefir Grains. To make the Water Kefir carbonated, pour a couple ounces of fruit juice into the strained water kefir you just strained. I've found Grape, Pomegranate, Apple and Cherry to work the best. I don't recommend citrus for this part, as it makes stringy yeast like things that are not tasty! Once you've added the juice, cover the jars tightly with an air tight lid and leave on the counter an additional 1-3 days before drinking or refrigerating. Repeat the process!

traditional GINGER ALE

ingredients

- A 1-2 inch piece of fresh ginger root, minced. Adjust this to taste. I use 2 inches as I prefer a stronger ginger taste.
- 1/2 cup of organic sugar or rapadura sugar. if using plain sugar, add 1 tablespoon molasses for flavor and minerals.
- 1/2 cup fresh lemon or lime juice
- 1/2 teaspoon sea salt or himalayan salt
- 8 cups of filtered (*chlorine free*) water
- 1/2 cup homemade ginger bug (*or can use 1/4 cup whey for a faster recipe though the flavor won't be quite as good.*)

directions

1. Make a "wort" for your ginger ale by placing 3 cups of the water, minced ginger root, sugar (and molasses if needed), and salt in a saucepan and bringing to a boil.

2. Simmer the mixture for about five minutes until sugar is dissolved and mixture starts to smell like ginger.

3. Remove from heat and add additional water. This should cool it but if not, allow to cool to room temperature before moving to the next step.

4. Add fresh lemon or lime juice and ginger bug (or whey).

5. Transfer to a 2 quart glass mason jar with a tight fitting (air-tight) lid. Stir well and put lid on.

6. Leave on the counter for 2-3 days until carbonated and transfer to the fridge where it will last indefinitely.

7. Watch this step carefully. Using whey will cause it to ferment more quickly and it will take less time. It should be bubble and should "hiss" like a soda when the lid is removed. This is very temperature dependent and the mixture may need to be burped or stirred during this fermentation time on the counter.

8. As with any traditional fermented drink, it is more of an art than a science as it depends on the strength of your culture, the temperature of your house and the sugar used. The final mixture should smell of ginger and slightly of yeast/fermentation and should be fizzy. Watch carefully that it doesn't become too carbonated as this will cause too much pressure and may result in an exploding jar!

9. The mixture can be strained and transferred to Grolsch style bottles before putting in the fridge.

10. Strain before drinking.

probiotic LEMONADE

ingredients

- Juice of 10 lemons or limes
- 1/4 cup sugar or sucanat
- 1 cup of whey
- 2.5 to 3 quarts of filtered water
- gallon size jar

directions

1 Pour the sugar into the gallon size glass jar and add just enough hot water to dissolve the sugar.

2 Add lemon juice and fill the jar about 3/4 full with filtered water.

3 Make sure the liquid is at room temp and add the whey.

4 Cover tightly and let sit on the counter for 2-3 days. The longer it sits, the less sugar in the final product.

5 After 2-3 days, keep in fridge and drink 4-6 ounces per day. The flavor will continue to develop in the fridge.

6 Since the sugar ferments out, it is rather tart. Add a couple drops of stevia if it is too tart for you!

electrolyte DRINKS

ingredients

- 1 quart of liquid (*options: green tea, herbal teas, coconut water, plain water, etc*)

- 1/8-1/4 teaspoon Himalayan sea salt (*regular table salt will work, but it doesn't have all the trace minerals*)

- 1/4 to 1/2 teaspoon crushed calcium magnesium tablets or powder (*optional*)

- 1/4 cup or more of juice (*optional*) - can use grape, apple, lemon, lime, pineapple, etc)

- 1-2 tablespoons sweetener (*optional*) - can use honey, stevia, etc. I suggest brewing stevia leaf into the base liquid for the most natural option.

directions

1. Brew tea if using or slightly warm base liquid

2. Add sea salt and calcium magnesium (if using)

3. Add juice and mix or shake well

4. Cool and store in fridge until ready to use

SuperFuel COFFEE

superfood vanilla latte

- 1 cup of brewed coffee or herbal coffee alternative
- 1 tablespoon of grass fed butter like Kalona or Kerrygold
- 1 tablespoon of coconut oil or MCT oil
- 1 tablespoon (*or more*) Collagen Hydrolysate (*work up slowly!*)
- 5 drops of vanilla stevia extract or 1/2 teaspoon pure vanilla extract

Brew coffee in a french press for best results, but any coffee will work. Place brewed coffee, butter, coconut oil/MCT, collagen and vanilla in a blender.Note: do not use a magic bullet or other closed in blender as it can crack or explode. Blend on high for 10-15 seconds until froth forms. Drink and enjoy.

salted caramel latte

- 1 cup of organic coffee, herbal coffee or chai tea
- 1 tablespoon coconut oil (or MCT Oil)
- 1 teaspoon organic grassfed salted butter
- sprinkle of Himalayan Salt
- 1/2 teaspoon vanilla
- 1 teaspoon of raw honey
- Optional: A sprinkle of sea salt and a drizzle of honey to top.

Brew coffee. Add all ingredients to a blender and blend on high for 15 seconds or until emulsified. Drink immediately. Enjoy!

basic superfood coffee

- 1 cup of organic coffee, herbal coffee or chai tea
- 1 tablespoon coconut oil *(or more, I usually put in 2-3 tablespoons)*
- 1 teaspoon organic grassfed unsalted butter
- 1/4 teaspoon vanilla
- a few drops of stevia extract *(optional)*

Put all ingredients in a blender or food processor. Mix on high speed for 20 seconds until frothy. Drink immediately and enjoy all the energy!

ingredients

- 1 cup raw organic almonds – soaked overnight (*this step reduces the level of phytates*)
- 4 cups pure filtered water
- vanilla bean (*optional*)
- dates, honey or stevia (*optional*)

directions

1. Soak almonds for at least 12 hours in pure water with 1/2 teaspoon sea salt. This is an important step as it breaks down the phytic acid and enzyme inhibitors and cultures beneficial enzymes in the almonds. (*side note: soaking nuts should be done before eating them as well. Soak nuts in salt water for 12 hours, rinse them, and dry in oven on lowest heat.*)

2. Rinse almonds well. Mix almonds with pure water in blender or Vitamix.

3. Blend several minutes until smooth and creamy. (*Warning: mixture will expand some, so make sure your blender is not full before starting it*)

4. Strain mixture into a large bowl through a sprout bag, cheese cloth or kitchen towel.

5. Put mixture back into blender with vanilla, soaked dates, or other sweetener.

6. Pour into glass jar or pitcher and store in fridge for up to one week.

note:

Save the pulp of the almonds, put on cookie sheet and dehydrate in oven on lowest heat until completely dry. Run through blender or food processor to make almond flour, which can be used in recipes in place of flour.

ingredients

- 4 cups of water
- 1.5-2 cups of unsweetened shredded coconut

directions

1. Heat water, but don't boil. It should be hot, but not scalding.

2. Put coconut in blender or Vitamix and add water. *(If all water won't fit, you can add the water in two batches.)*

3. Blend on high for several minutes until thick and creamy.

4. Pour through a mesh colander first to get most of the coconut out, and then squeeze through a towel or several thicknesses of cheesecloth to get remaining pieces of coconut out.

5. If you have to split the water, put all the coconut that you strained out back in the blender, add the remaining water, and repeat.

6. Flavor options- add in after all coconut has been strained out: 1/2 teaspoon vanilla extract, 1/2 cup fresh or frozen strawberries, 2 teaspoons cocoa powder + 1/2 teaspoon vanilla.

7. Drink immediately or store in the fridge. Should be used in 3-4 days after making for best flavor and texture. Since there are no preservatives or fillers, the "cream" of the coconut milk may separate on the top if stored in the fridge. Just shake or stir before using.

ingredients

- 1 cup already-brewed Kombucha, preferably with natural fruit/juice added and second ferment completed

- 1/4 to 1/2 cup rehydrated chia seed gel - to make: add 1 part chia seeds to 4 parts warm water (*I usually mix 1/4 cup seeds with 1 cup warm water*), stir well, put lid on and leave in fridge at least a few hours.

directions

1 Put as much rehydrated chia seed gel as desired in a cup or bottle.

2 Add 1 cup or more of kombucha and stir well to incorporate.

3 Drink and enjoy!

10 HERBAL TEAS

chamomile

Chamomile flower tea is one of the most consumed teas in the world behind regular black tea. Chamomile flowers have a naturally sweet taste with a hint of an apple flavor. Chamomile is a good herbal source of Magnesium, and is known as a soothing and relaxing herb.

It makes an excellent in the evening or in times of stress because of its mildly sedative and soothing properties. It is an excellent herb for children and can even be an effective remedy for pink eye.

Chamomile can be made into a tincture for a more potent effect and to extend shelf life.

mint

Mint tea is probably second to Chamomile in popularity among herbal teas. Peppermint tea soothes the digestive track and is helpful for heartburn, nausea and indigestion. I drink it daily in early pregnancy to help alleviate nausea and use it in a homemade digestive tincture.

While it is especially helpful during illness, Peppermint is a delicious tea anytime and can be consumed alone or with other herbs to help increase their effectiveness.

raspberry leaf

Raspberry leaf is my favorite tea and I drink it daily. It is highly nutritious and especially beneficial for women as it helps balance hormones and is good for the skin. It is often consumed during pregnancy as it can strengthen the uterus and is a good source of Magnesium, Potassium, and B-Vitamins (all important during pregnancy).

Raspberry Leaf Tea has a taste similar to regular black tea and can be combined with Stevia leaf to make a naturally sweet tea. I drink it hot in the winer and cold during the summer months and my kids like it iced (and sometimes with chia seeds in it). Herbalists often recommend Raspberry Leaf tea or tincture to women suffering from infertility, PCOS, endometriosis, or painful menses.

sleep easy blend

My go-to tea when I am having trouble sleeping is an equal mixture of Chamomile, Mint, and Catnip herbs. Catnip has natural relaxing and soothing properties. It is one of the ingredients in my Sweet Dreams Sleep Tincture, which is great at helping kids relax and sleep better, especially during illness.

I mix a teaspoon each of Chamomile, Mint, and Catnip herbs in a glass of water for a relaxing nighttime tea that is also great during illness. This same mixture can be used to fill a homemade eye pillow to aid in sleep as well.

lavender tea

Lavender is my favorite scent and essential oil but it is too strong to be used alone in a tea. My favorite Lavender Tea recipe is:

- 1/2 cup Mint Leaf

- 2 Tablespoons Dried Lavender

- 2 Tablespoons Stevia (optional)

Mix all and store in an air-tight container. Use 1-2 teaspoons per cup of water to make hot or iced tea.

chai tea

Chai tea is a favorite around our house and we usually make it with Raspberry Leaf tea instead of black tea and with coconut milk instead of regular milk. There are many variations of chai tea recipes and with a little experimenting, you can find the one that you like best. Here is my basic recipe to give you some ideas.

When I don't feel like making my own, I love this caffeine free Firefly Chai that is slightly sweeter than regular Chai and is great for nighttime. If you add a little chamomile and catnip to it, it is a delicious evening drink for kids.

herbal coffee

Have trouble kicking the coffee habit? While I still love coffee once in a while, an herbal coffee is a great alternative without the caffeine. My favorite one packs a powerful nutritional punch too with maca powder and dandelion root!

stomach soother

For stomach aches or for those prone to digestive troubles, this tea is very calming. The recipe is also very easy:

- 2 teaspoons mint leaf

- 1/2 teaspoon fennel seeds

- pinch of dried ginger *(optional)*

Pour 1 cup of boiling water over it, steep, covered for 5 minutes and consume. You can also add some grass-fed gelatin powder *(about a tablespoon)* for a long-lasting soothing effect.

During pregnancy I drink a special tea that helps keep nausea and digestive troubles at bay and also helps strengthen the uterus. The nettle also provides Vitamin K, an essential nutrient for pregnancy and birth to help with clotting.

Many women report having easier and faster labors from using this tea, though my labors are typically 24+ hours even though I go natural, so I may not be the best example! This tea is delicious anytime, but especially during pregnancy.

- 4 cups raspberry leaf
- 1/2 cup mint leaf
- 1/4 cup stevia leaf
- 1 cup nettle leaf

Mix and use 1 tablespoon to brew by the glass or 1 cup to brew by the gallon. Add more or less stevia to taste. Enjoy!

kombucha tea

This herbal tea is consumed cold and requires a culture to make but it is packed with vitamins and probiotics. It is made with regular black tea, though I'm experimenting with making it with coffee as well. Kombucha is a slightly sweet, slightly tangy drink that can be made fizzy like soda if a secondary fermentation is done.

Many people report extra energy and more mental clarity from drinking Kombucha.

herbal WASSAIL

ingredients

- 1/2 gallon apple cider
- 1 quart freshly brewed tea made with red raspberry leaf (*3 parts*), alfalfa (*2 parts*), nettle (*1 part*), and dandelion (*1 part*)
- 2 cups pineapple juice
- 2 cups cranberry juice
- 8 cinnamon sticks
- 3 organic oranges, cloved

directions

1   Peel oranges, section, and put 1 clove in the middle of each section.

2   Mix juices and tea in large pot (*or reduce quantities and put in crock pot*).

3   Put cinnamon sticks and oranges in the mixture.

4   Simmer in large pot for one hour and serve. Can also be kept in crock pot all day.

ingredients

- 1 can of coconut milk or 2 cups of homemade (*or 2 cups of hot but not boiling water and 3 tablespoons shredded coconut if you have a Vitamix or high powered blender*)

- 1 teaspoon turmeric

- 1 teaspoon cinnamon

- 1 tablespoon honey or maple syrup or to taste

- pinch of cayenne pepper (*optional*)

directions

1 If you have a Vitamix or other good blender, just dump hot water, shredded coconut, Turmeric, Cinnamon, honey/maple syrup and cayenne into the blender and blend for 2 minutes.

2 If not, heat the coconut milk on the stove until hot but not boiling then add the other ingredients and stir well. You can also heat the coconut milk and then add all ingredients to a blender for a smoother version.

sources:

Grains:

Carrera-Bastos, P., et al. (2011). The western diet and lifestyle and diseases of civilization. Dovepress, 2011(2). 15-35. http://dx.doi.org/10.2147/RRCC.S16919

Cordain, L. (1999). Cereal grains: Humanity's double-edged sword. In Simopoulos, A. (ed), Evolutionary aspects of nutrition and health: Diet exercise, genetics and chronic disease. World Review of Nutrition and Diet, 84, 19-73. Retrieved from http://www.direct-ms.org/pdf/EvolutionPaleolithic/Cereal%20Sword.pdf

Fontes-Villalba, M., Carrera-Bastos, P., & Cordain. L. (2014, February). African hominin stable isotopic data do not necessarily indicate grass consumption. PNAS Early Edition, Retrieved from http://2iefwlm3f1n81i891vivh3mx7.wpengine.netdna-cdn.com/wp-content/uploads/2014/02/African+Hominin+Stable+Isotopic+Data+Do+Not+Necessarily+Indicate+Grass+Consumption+The+Paleo+Diet.pdf

Frassetto, L. A., Schloetter, M., Mietus-Synder, M., Morris Jr., R.C. & Sebastian, A. (2009). Metabolic and physiologic improvements from consuming a paleolithic, hunter-gatherer type diet. European Journal of Clinical Nutrition, 63, 947–955. Retrieved from http://www.ncbi.nlm.nih.gov/pubmed/19209185

Freed, D. L. J. (1999). Do dietary lectins cause disease? British Medical Journal, 318(7190), 1023-1024. Retrieved from http://www.ncbi.nlm.nih.gov/pmc/articles/PMC1115436/?tool=pubmed

Greger, J. L. (1999). Nondigestible carbohydrates and mineral bioavailability. Journal of Nutrition, 129(7), 1434S-1435S. Retrieved from http://jn.nutrition.org/content/129/7/1434S.abstract

Jönsson, T., Olsson, S., Ahrén, B., Bøg-Hansen, T. C., Dole, A., & Lindeberg, S. (2005). Agrarian diet and diseases of affluence – Do evolutionary novel dietary lectins cause leptin resistance? BMC Endocrine Disorders, 5, 10. doi:10.1186/1472-6823-5-10

Lindeberg S, et al. (2007). A Palaeolithic diet improves glucose tolerance more than a Mediterranean-like diet in individuals with ischaemic heart disease. Diabetologia, 50(9), 1795-1807. Retrieved from http://www.ncbi.nlm.nih.gov/pubmed/17583796

Lund University. (2007, June 28). Original Human 'Stone Age' Diet Is Good For People With Diabetes, Study Finds. ScienceDaily. Retrieved from www.sciencedaily.com/releases/2007/06/070627225459.htm

Medical College of Georgia. (2006, August 23). Scientists Learn More About How Roughage Keeps You 'Regular'. ScienceDaily. Retrieved from http://www.sciencedaily.com/releases/2006/08/060823093156.htm

Melnik, B. C., Schmitz, G., John, S. M., Carrera-Bastos, P., Lindeberg, S. & Cordain, L. (2013). Metabolic effects of milk protein intake strongly depend on pre-existing metabolic and exercise status. Nutrition & Metabolism, 10:60. doi:10.1186/1743-7075-10-60

O'Keefe, Jr., J. H., Cordain, L., Jones, P. G., & Abuissa, H., (2006). Coronary artery disease prognosis and C-Reactive Protein levels improve in proportion to percent lowering of low-density lipoprotein. American Journal of Cardiology, 98, 135-139. Retrieved from http://2iefwlm3f1n81i891vivh3mx7.wpengine.netdna-cdn.com/wp-content/uploads/2014/06/Coronary+Artery+Disease+Prognosis+and+C+Reactive+Protein-Levels+Improve+in+Proportion+to+Percent+Lowering+of+Low+Density+Lipoprotein.pdf

Suny Downstate Medical Center. (2007, December 4). Low-carb diet reduces inflammation and blood saturated fat in metabolic syndrome. ScienceDaily. Retrieved from www.sciencedaily.com/releases/2007/12/071203091236.htm

Westman, E. C., et al. (2007). Low-carbohydrate nutrition and metabolism. American Journal of Clinical Nutrition, 86(2), 276-284. Retrieved from http://ajcn.nutrition.org/content/86/2/276.full

Zanchi, C., Di Leo, G., Ronfani, L., Martelossi, S., Not, T., Ventura, A. (2008). Bone metabolism in celiac disease. Journal of Pediatrics, 152(2), 262-265. doi:10.1016/j.jpeds.2008.03.003

Vegetable Oils:
Calder, P. C. (2006). n–3 Polyunsaturated fatty acids, inflammation, and inflammatory diseases. American Journal of Clinical Nutrition, 83(6), S1505-S1519. Retrieved from http://ajcn.nutrition.org/content/83/6/S1505.short

Christakis, G., Rinzler, S. H., Archer, M, & Kraus, A. (1966). Effect of the anti-coronary club program on coronary heart disease risk-factor status. Journal of the American Medical Association. 198(6), 597-604. doi:10.1001/jama.1966.03110190079022

Cordain, L. (1998) Atherogenic potential of peanut oil-based monounsaturated fatty acids diets. (Letter to the Editor). Lipids, 33(2), 229-230. Retrieved from https://s3.amazonaws.com/paleodietevo2/research/Atherogenic+Potential+of+Peanut+Oil+Based+Monounsaturated+Fatty+Acids+Diet+The+Paleo+Diet.pdf

Cordain, L., (2002). The nutritional characteristics of a contemporary diet based upon paleolithic food groups. Journal of the American Nutraceutical Association, 5(3), 15-24. Retrieved from https://s3.amazonaws.com/paleodietevo2/research/The+Nutritional+Characteristics+of+a+Contemporary+Diet+Based+Upon+Paleolithic+Food+Groups+The+Paleo+Diet.pdf

Cordain, L. & Hickey, M. S. (2006) Ultraviolet radiation represents an evolutionary selective pressure for the south-to-north gradient of the MTHFR 677TT genotype. American Journal of Clinical Nutrition, 84(5), 1243. Retrieved from http://ajcn.nutrition.org/content/84/5/1243.full

Dayton, S., Pearce, M. L., Hashimoto, S., Dixon, W. J., & Tomiyasu, U. (1969). A controlled clinical trial of a diet high in unsaturated fat in preventing complications of atherosclerosis. Circulation, 40, 11-1-11-63. doi:10.1161/01.CIR.40.1S2.II-1

Eaton, S. B., Eaton III, S. B., Sinclair, A. J., Cordain, L., & Mann, N. J. (1998). Dietary iIntake of long-chain polyunsaturated fatty acids during the paleolithic. In Simopoulos, A.P. (ed), The return of omega 3 fatty acids into the food supply: I. Land-based animal food products and their health effects. World Review of Nutrition and Diet, 83, 12-23. Retrieved from http://www.direct-ms.org/pdf/EvolutionPaleolithic/Long%20chain%20fatty%20acids.pdf

Frantz, Jr., I. D., et al. (1989). Test of effect of lipid lowering by diet on cardiovascular risk: The Minnesota Coronary Survey. Arteriosclerosis, Thrombosis, and Vascular Biology, 9, 129-135. doi:10.1161/01.ATV.9.1.129

Ghosh, S., Novak, E. M., Innis, S. M. (2007). Cardiac proinflammatory pathways are altered with different dietary n-6 linoleic to n-3 α-linolenic acid ratios in normal, fat-fed pigs. American Journal of Physiology - Heart and Circulatory Physiology, 293, H2919-H2927. doi:10.1152/ajpheart.00324.2007

Guyenet, S. (2011, August 21). Seed oils and body fatness-- A problematic revisit. Retrieved from http://wholehealthsource.blogspot.com/2011/08/seed-oils-and-body-fatness-problematic.html

Haigh, M., & Heady, J. A. (1968). Controlled trial of soya-bean oil in myocardial infarction. Lancet, 2(7570), 693-699. Retrieved from http://www.thelancet.com/journals/lancet/article/PIIS0140-6736%2868%2990746-0/abstract

Hibbeln, J. R., Nieminen, L. R, & Lands, W. E. (2004). Increasing homicide rates and linoleic acid consumption among five Western countries, 1961-2000. Lipids, 39(12), 1207-1213. Retrieved from http://www.ncbi.nlm.nih.gov/pubmed/15736917

Hibbeln, J. R., Nieminen, L. R. G., Blasbalg, T. L., Riggs, J. A., & Lands, W. E. M. (2006). Healthy intakes of n–3 and n–6 fatty acids: estimations considering worldwide diversity. American Journal of Clinical Nutrition, 83(6), S1483-S1493. Retrieved from http://ajcn.nutrition.org/content/83/6/S1483.abstract

Kiecolt-Glaser, J. K., Belury, M. A., Porter, K., Beversdorf, D. Q., Lemeshow, S., & Glaser, R. (2007). Depressive symptoms, omega -6:omega-3 fatty acids, and inflammation in older adults. Psychosomatic Medicine, 69(3), 217-224. doi:10.1097/PSY.0b013e3180313a45

Lands, W. E. M. (2001). Biochemistry and physiology of eicosanoid precursors in cell membranes. European Heart Journal Supplements, 3(D), D22-D25. doi:10.1016/S1520-765X(01)90114-2

Leren, P. (1968). The effect of plasma-cholesterol-lowering diet in male survivors of myocardial infarction: A controlled clinical trial. Bulletin of the New York Academy of Medicine, 44(8), 1012-1020. Retrieved from http://www.ncbi.nlm.nih.gov/pmc/articles/PMC1750292/

Lindenberg, S., Cordain, L., & Eaton, S. B. (2003). Biological and clinical potential of a palaeolithic diet. Journal of Nutritional & Environmental Medicine, 13(3), 149–160. Retrieved from https://s3.amazonaws.com/paleodietevo2/research/Biological+and+Clinical+Potential+of+a+Palaeolithic+Diet+The+Paleo+Diet.pdf

de Lorgeril, M., & Salen, P. (2012). New insights into the health effects of dietary saturated and omega-6 and omega-3 polyunsaturated fatty acids. BMC Medicine, 10, 50. doi:10.1186/1741-7015-10-50

Nair, U., Bartsch, H., & Nair, J. (2007). Lipid peroxidation-induced DNA damage in cancer-prone inflammatory diseases: a review of published adduct types and levels in humans. Free Radical Biology and Medicine, 43(8), 1109-1120. Retrieved from http://www.ncbi.nlm.nih.gov/pubmed/17854706

Ramsden, C. E., Hibbeln, J. R., Majchrzak, S. F., & Davis, J.M. (2010). n-6 fatty acid-specific and mixed polyunsaturate dietary interventions have different effects on CHD risk: a meta-analysis of randomised controlled trials. British Journal of Nutrition, 104(11), 1586-1600. doi:10.1017/S0007114510004010

Rose, G. A., Thomson, W. B., and Williams, R. T. (1965). Corn oil in treatment of ischaemic heart disease. British Medical Journal, 1(5449), 1531-1533. Retrieved from http://www.ncbi.nlm.nih.gov/pmc/articles/PMC2166702/

Simopoulos, A. P. (2002). The importance of the ratio of omega-6/omega-3 essential fatty acids. Biomedicine & Pharmacotherapy, 56(8), 365-379. doi:10.1016/S0753-3322(02)00253-6

Simopoulos, A. P. (2006). Evolutionary aspects of diet, the omega-6/omega-3 ratio and genetic variation: nutritional implications for chronic diseases. Biomedicine & Pharmacotherapy, 60(9), 502-507. doi:10.1016/j.biopha.2006.07.080

Siri-Tarino, P. W., Sun, Q., Hu, F. B., & Krauss, R. M. (2010). Meta-analysis of prospective cohort studies evaluating the association of saturated fat with cardiovascular disease. American Journal of Clinical Nutrition, 91(3), 535-546. doi:10.3945/ajcn.2009.27725

University of Toronto. (2013, November 11). Some 'healthy' vegetable oils may actually increase risk of heart disease. ScienceDaily. Retrieved from www.sciencedaily.com/releases/2013/11/131111122105.htm

Sugar:

Ackerman, Z., et al. (2005). Fructose-induced fatty liver disease: Hepatic effects of blood pressure and plasma triglyceride reduction. Hypertension, 45, 1012-1018. doi:10.1161/01. HYP.0000164570.20420.67

Banks, W. A., et al. (2004). Triglycerides induce leptin resistance at the blood-brain barrier. Diabetes, 53(5), 1253-1260. Retrieved from http://www.ncbi.nlm.nih.gov/pubmed/15111494

Conlee, R. K., Lawler, R. M., & Ross, P. E. (1987). Effects of glucose or fructose feeding on glycogen repletion in muscle and liver after exercise or fasting. Annals of Nutrition & Metabolism, 31(2), 126-132. Retrieved from http://www.ncbi.nlm.nih.gov/pubmed/3592616

Faeh, D., Minehira, K., Schwarz, J., Periasamy, R., Park, S., & Tappy, L. (2005). Effect of fructose overfeeding and fish oil administration on hepatic de novo lipogenesis and insulin sensitivity in healthy men. Diabetes, 54(7), 1907-1913. doi:10.2337/diabetes.54.7.1907

Ouyang, X., et al. (2008). Fructose consumption as a risk factor for non-alcoholic fatty liver disease. Journal of Hepatology, 48(6), 993-999. http://dx.doi.org/10.1016/j.jhep.2008.02.011

Rada, P., Avena, N. M., Hoebel, B. H. (2005). Daily bingeing on sugar repeatedly releases dopamine in the accumbens shell. Neuroscience, 134(3), 737-744. doi:10.1016/j.neuroscience.2005.04.043

Stanhope, K. L., et al. (2009). Consuming fructose-sweetened, not glucose-sweetened, beverages increases visceral adiposity and lipids and decreases insulin sensitivity in overweight/obese humans. Journal of Clinical Investigation, 119(5), 1322-1334. Retrieved from http://www.ncbi.nlm.nih.gov/pmc/articles/PMC2673878/

Zelber-Sagi, S., et al. (2007). Long term nutritional intake and the risk for non-alcoholic fatty liver disease (NAFLD): A population based study. Journal of Hepatology, 47(5), 711-717. http://dx.doi.org/10.1016/j.jhep.2007.06.020

index: